Great Recipes
FROM AROUND
the World

Great Recipes
FROM AROUND
the World

S A R A H   G A T E S

OVER 130 EASY-TO-COOK
INTERNATIONAL DISHES

A.G. City Books

First published in 1995 by A.G. City Books

© Anness Publishing Limited 1994

A.G. City Books
655 The Queensway, Unit 8
Peterborough, ON.
K9J 7M1
Canada
Telephone: (705) 741-1385
Fax: (705) 741-1185

Publisher: Joanna Lorenz
Senior Cookery Editor: Linda Fraser
Designer: Tony Paine
Photographer: Steve Baxter
Food for Photography: Wendy Lee
Props Stylist: Blake Minton

Printed and bound in Singapore

CONTENTS

SOUPS

Cooking up a selection of soups from around the world was like taking a world cruise without moving an inch from the cooker! The kitchen became filled with a glorious succession of the smells of herbs, spices, and savoury ingredients that go into creating the unique flavours of the popular classics. This selection of hot and cold favourites will give you a taste of the countries they come from. From the sunny Mediterranean comes a hearty Italian Minestrone topped with Pesto Toasts. The flavours of the Far East are captured in a delicious mildly spicy Chicken Soup from Thailand. There's a tasty Rich Tomato Soup from Great Britain for all tomato lovers, and the New England Spiced Pumpkin Soup is the perfect winter warmer.

MINESTRONE WITH PESTO TOASTS

This Italian mixed vegetable soup comes originally from Genoa, but the vegetables vary from region to region. This is also a great way to use up left-over vegetables.

INGREDIENTS

Serves 4
30ml/2 tbsp olive oil
2 garlic cloves, crushed
1 onion, halved and sliced
225g/8oz/2 cups diced lean bacon
2 small courgettes, quartered
  and sliced
50g/2oz/½ cup French beans, chopped
2 small carrots, diced
2 celery sticks, finely chopped
bouquet garni
50g/2oz/½ cup short cut macaroni
50g/2oz/½ cup frozen peas
200g/7oz can red kidney beans, drained
  and rinsed
50g/2oz/1 cup shredded green cabbage
4 tomatoes, skinned and seeded
salt and black pepper

For the toasts
8 slices French bread
15ml/1 tbsp ready-made pesto sauce
15ml/1 tbsp grated Parmesan cheese

1 Heat the oil in a large pan and gently fry the garlic and onions for 5 minutes, until just softened. Add the bacon, courgettes, French beans, carrots and celery to the pan and stir-fry for a further 3 minutes.

2 Pour 1.1 litres/2 pints/5 cups of cold water over the vegetables and add the bouquet garni. Cover the pan and simmer for 25 minutes.

3 Add the macaroni, peas and kidney beans and cook for 8 minutes. Then add the cabbage and tomatoes and cook for a further 5 minutes.

4 Meanwhile, spread the bread slices with the pesto, sprinkle a little Parmesan over each one and brown lightly under a hot grill.

5 Remove the bouquet garni, season the soup and serve with the toasts.

> **COOK'S TIP**
> If you like, to appeal to children, you could replace the macaroni with coloured pasta shapes such as shells, twists or bows.

CORN AND SHELLFISH CHOWDER

Chowder comes from the French word *chaudron* meaning a large cooking pot. This is what the fishermen on the east coast of North America used for boiling up whatever was left over from their catch for supper.

INGREDIENTS

Serves 4

25g/1oz/2 tbsp butter
1 small onion, chopped
340g/12oz can sweetcorn, drained
600ml/1 pint/2½ cups milk
175g/6oz can white crabmeat, drained and flaked
115g/4oz/1 cup peeled cooked prawns
2 spring onions, finely chopped
150ml/¼ pint/⅔ cup single cream
pinch of cayenne pepper
salt and black pepper
4 whole prawns in shells, to garnish

1 Melt the butter in a large saucepan and gently fry the onion for 4–5 minutes, until softened.

2 Reserve 30ml/2 tbsp of the sweetcorn for the garnish and add the remainder to the pan with the milk. Bring the soup to the boil, then reduce the heat, cover the pan and simmer over a low heat for 5 minutes.

3 Pour the soup, in batches if necessary, into a blender or food processor and whizz until smooth.

4 Return the soup to the pan and stir in the crabmeat, prawns, spring onions, cream and cayenne pepper. Reheat gently over a low heat.

5 Meanwhile, place the reserved sweetcorn kernels in a small frying pan without oil and dry-fry over a medium heat until golden and toasted.

6 Season the soup well and serve each bowlful topped with a few of the toasted kernels and a whole prawn.

RICH TOMATO SOUP

A great British favourite – this fresh soup tastes so much nicer than the canned version. Make sure you use good-flavoured, ripe tomatoes, or home-grown.

INGREDIENTS

Serves 4

1kg/2lb (about 12 medium) tomatoes
15ml/1 tbsp olive oil
1 large onion, chopped
1 garlic clove, crushed
1 potato, chopped
15ml/1 tbsp tomato purée
5ml/1 tsp caster sugar
salt and black pepper
60ml/4 tbsp fromage frais
fresh chervil sprigs, to garnish

1 Place the tomatoes in a large heatproof bowl. Cover them with boiling water and leave to stand for about 1–2 minutes.

2 Heat the olive oil in a large pan and add the onion, garlic and potato. Fry gently for about 5 minutes, until the onion has softened.

3 Meanwhile, drain the hot water from the tomatoes, peel off the skins then halve the tomatoes and remove the cores. Chop the tomato flesh and add to the pan with the seeds, any juice and the tomato purée.

4 Pour over 300ml/½ pint/1¼ cups boiling water, stir, then cover and simmer gently for about 15 minutes, until the potato is soft.

5 Purée the soup in batches in a blender or food processor until smooth. Return the soup to the saucepan, add the sugar, season well and heat through. Serve in bowls with a dollop of fromage frais and the sprigs of fresh chervil.

FRENCH ONION SOUP

INGREDIENTS

Serves 4

25g/1oz/2 tbsp butter
15ml/1 tbsp oil
3 large onions, thinly sliced
5ml/1 tsp soft brown sugar
15ml/1 tbsp plain flour
2 x 300g/10oz cans condensed beef
  consommé
30ml/2 tbsp medium sherry
10ml/2 tsp Worcestershire sauce
8 slices French bread
15ml/1 tbsp French coarse-grained
  mustard
75g/3oz/1 cup Gruyère cheese, grated
salt and black pepper
15ml/1 tbsp chopped fresh parsley, to
  garnish

1 Heat the butter and oil in a large saucepan and add the onions and brown sugar. Cook gently for about 20 minutes, stirring occasionally, until the onions start to turn golden brown.

2 Stir in the flour and cook for a further 2 minutes. Pour in the consommé, plus two cans of water, then add the sherry and Worcestershire sauce. Season well, cover and simmer gently for a further 25–30 minutes.

3 Preheat the grill and just before serving, toast the bread lightly on both sides. Spread one side of each slice with the mustard and top with the grated cheese. Grill the toasts until bubbling and golden.

4 Ladle the soup into bowls. Pop two croûtons on top of each bowl of soup and garnish with chopped fresh parsley. Serve at once.

CHILLED LEEK AND POTATO SOUP

This creamy, chilled soup is a version of the *Vichyssoise* originally created by a French chef at the Ritz Carlton Hotel in New York to celebrate the opening of the roof gardens.

INGREDIENTS

Serves 4

25g/1oz/2 tbsp butter
15ml/1 tbsp vegetable oil
1 small onion, chopped
3 leeks, sliced
2 potatoes, diced
600ml/1 pint/2½ cups vegetable stock
300ml/½ pint/1¼ cups milk
45ml/3 tbsp single cream
a little extra milk (optional)
salt and black pepper
60ml/4 tbsp natural yogurt and snipped chives, to garnish

1 Heat the butter and oil in a large saucepan and add the onion, leeks and potatoes. Cover and simmer for 15 minutes, stirring occasionally. Stir in the stock and milk and simmer for 10 minutes, until the potatoes are tender.

2 Ladle the vegetables and liquid into a blender or food processor in batches and purée until smooth. Return the soup to the pan, stir in the cream and season well.

3 Leave the soup to cool, and then chill for 3–4 hours, or until really cold. You may need to add a little extra milk to thin the soup down as it will thicken slightly as it cools.

4 Serve the chilled soup in individual bowls, topped with a spoonful of natural yogurt and a sprinkling of snipped fresh chives.

CURRIED PARSNIP SOUP

The spices impart a delicious, mild curry flavour which brings back memories of the Raj.

INGREDIENTS

Serves 4

25g/1oz/2 tbsp butter
1 garlic clove, crushed
1 onion, chopped
5ml/1 tsp ground cumin
5ml/1 tsp ground coriander
450g/1lb (about 4) parsnips, sliced
10ml/2 tsp medium curry paste
450ml/¾ pint/1⅞ cups chicken stock
450ml/¾ pint/1⅞ cups milk
60ml/4 tbsp soured cream
squeeze of lemon juice
salt and black pepper
fresh coriander sprigs, to garnish
ready-made garlic and coriander naan bread, to serve

1 Heat the butter in a large saucepan and add the garlic and onion. Fry gently for 4–5 minutes, until lightly golden. Stir in the spices and cook for a further 1–2 minutes.

2 Add the parsnips and stir until well coated with the butter, then stir in the curry paste, followed by the stock. Cover the pan and simmer for 15 minutes, until the parsnips are tender.

3 Ladle the soup into a blender or food processor and whizz until smooth. Return to the pan and stir in the milk. Heat gently for 2–3 minutes, then add 30ml/2 tbsp of the soured cream and the lemon juice. Season well.

4 Serve in bowls topped with spoonfuls of the remaining soured cream and the fresh coriander accompanied by the naan bread.

THAI CHICKEN SOUP

Serves 4

15ml/1 tbsp vegetable oil
1 garlic clove, finely chopped
2 x 175g/6oz boned chicken breasts,
  skinned and chopped
2.5ml/½ tsp ground turmeric
1.25ml/¼ tsp hot chilli powder
75g/3oz creamed coconut
900ml/1½ pints/3¾ cups hot chicken
  stock
30ml/2 tbsp lemon or lime juice
30ml/2 tbsp crunchy peanut butter
50g/2oz/1 cup thread egg noodles,
  broken into small pieces
15ml/1 tbsp spring onions, finely
  chopped
15ml/1 tbsp chopped fresh coriander
salt and black pepper
30ml/2 tbsp desiccated coconut and
  ½ fresh red chilli, seeded and finely
  chopped, to garnish

1 Heat the oil in a large pan and fry the garlic for 1 minute until lightly golden. Add the chicken and spices and stir-fry for a further 3–4 minutes.

2 Crumble the creamed coconut into the hot chicken stock and stir until dissolved. Pour on to the chicken and add the lemon juice, peanut butter and egg noodles.

3 Cover and simmer for about 15 minutes. Add the spring onions and fresh coriander, then season well and cook for a further 5 minutes.

4 Meanwhile, place the coconut and chilli in a small frying pan and heat for 2–3 minutes, stirring frequently, until the coconut is lightly browned.

5 Serve the soup in bowls sprinkled with the fried coconut and chilli.

NEW ENGLAND SPICED PUMPKIN SOUP

Serves 4

25g/1oz/2 tbsp butter
1 onion, finely chopped
1 small garlic clove, crushed
15ml/1 tbsp plain flour
pinch of grated nutmeg
2.5ml/½ tsp ground cinnamon
350g/12oz/3 cups pumpkin, seeded,
  peeled and cubed
600ml/1 pint/2½ cups chicken stock
150ml/¼ pint/⅔ cup orange juice
5ml/1 tsp brown sugar
15ml/1 tbsp vegetable oil
2 slices Granary bread without crusts
30ml/2 tbsp sunflower seeds
salt and black pepper

1 Heat the butter in a large saucepan, add the onions and garlic and fry gently for 4–5 minutes, until softened.

2 Stir in the flour, spices and pumpkin, then cover and cook gently for 6 minutes, stirring occasionally.

3 Pour in the chicken stock and orange juice and add the brown sugar. Cover and bring to the boil, then reduce the heat and simmer for 20 minutes, until the pumpkin has softened.

4 Pour half of the mixture into a blender or food processor and whizz until smooth. Return the soup to the pan with the remaining chunky mixture, stirring constantly. Season well and heat through.

5 Meanwhile, make the croûtons. Heat the oil in a frying pan, cut the bread into cubes and fry gently until just beginning to brown. Add the sunflower seeds and fry for 1–2 minutes. Drain the croûtons on kitchen paper.

6 Serve the soup hot with a few of the croûtons scattered over the top. Serve the rest separately.

STARTERS AND SNACKS

How often have you set out to prepare a meal and not known what to start with, or felt like eating something deliciously different and run out of inspiration? This section offers you a globetrotter's range of recipes. There are ideal dinner party starters, like the delicious Pork and Prawn Toasts from the Far East, and the French Goats' Cheese Salad, as well as filling family snacks like the Tex-Mex Baked Potatoes with Chilli, Mediterranean Garlic Toast, or wedges of hot Spanish Omelette. Mexican Dip with Chilli Chips makes the perfect speedy snack or starter, and when light lunches are called for either Golden Cheese Puffs served with a salad or Kansas City Fritters with tomato salsa are the ideal answer.

INDIAN CURRIED LAMB SAMOSAS

INGREDIENTS

Serves 4

15ml/1 tbsp oil
1 garlic clove, crushed
175g/6oz minced lamb
4 spring onions, finely chopped
10ml/2 tsp medium curry paste
4 ready-to-eat dried apricots, chopped
1 small potato, diced
10ml/2 tsp apricot chutney
30ml/2 tbsp frozen peas
a good squeeze of lemon juice
15ml/1 tbsp fresh chopped coriander
225g/8oz puff pastry
beaten egg, to glaze
5ml/1 tsp cumin seeds
salt and black pepper
45ml/3 tbsp natural yogurt and 15ml/
* 1 tbsp chopped fresh mint, to serve*
fresh mint sprigs, to garnish

1 Preheat the oven to 220°C/425°F/ Gas 7 and dampen a large, non-stick baking sheet.

2 Heat the oil in a frying pan and fry the garlic for 30 seconds, then add the minced lamb. Continue frying for about 5 minutes, stirring frequently until the meat is well browned.

3 Stir in the spring onions, curry paste, apricots and potato, and cook for 2–3 minutes. Add the apricot chutney, peas and 60ml/4 tbsp water. Cover and simmer for 10 minutes, stirring occasionally. Stir in the lemon juice and chopped coriander, season, remove from the heat and leave to cool.

4 On a floured surface, roll out the pastry and cut into four 15cm/6in squares. Place a quarter of the curry mixture in the centre of each pastry square and brush the edges with beaten egg. Fold over to make a triangle and seal the edges. Knock up the edges with the back of a knife and make a small slit in the top of each.

5 Brush each samosa with beaten egg and sprinkle over the cumin seeds. Place on the damp baking sheet and bake for 20 minutes. Serve with yogurt and mint and garnish with mint sprigs.

MEXICAN DIP WITH CHILLI CHIPS

INGREDIENTS

Serves 4
2 medium ripe avocados
juice of 1 lime
½ small onion, finely chopped
½ red chilli, seeded and finely chopped
3 tomatoes, skinned, seeded and
  chopped
30ml/2 tbsp chopped fresh coriander
30ml/2 tbsp soured cream
salt and black pepper
15ml/1 tbsp soured cream and a pinch
  of cayenne pepper, to garnish

For the chips
150g/5oz bag tortilla chips
30ml/2 tbsp finely grated mature
  Cheddar cheese
1.25ml/¼tsp chilli powder
10ml/2 tbsp chopped fresh parsley

1 Halve and stone the avocados and remove the flesh with a spoon, scraping the shells well.

2 Place the flesh in a blender or food processor with the remaining ingredients and pulse until fairly smooth. Transfer to a bowl, cover and chill.

3 Meanwhile, preheat the grill, then scatter the tortilla chips over a baking sheet. Mix the grated cheese with the chilli powder, sprinkle over the chips and grill for 1–2 minutes, until the cheese has melted.

4 Remove the avocado dip from the fridge, top with the soured cream and sprinkle with cayenne pepper. Serve the bowl on a plate surrounded by the tortilla chips sprinkled with the fresh parsley.

PORK AND PRAWN TOASTS

A popular starter in China and Thailand. Serve the toasts piping hot with a bowl of sweet chilli dipping sauce.

INGREDIENTS

Serves 4
115g/4oz minced pork
115g/4oz/1 cup peeled cooked prawns
1 garlic clove, crushed
2 spring onions, finely chopped
30ml/2 tbsp chopped fresh coriander
1 egg white, lightly beaten
5ml/1 tsp light soy sauce
5ml/1 tsp grated lemon rind
4 slices white bread, crusts removed
60ml/4 tbsp sesame seeds
oil, for frying
lemon wedges, to serve
fresh coriander sprigs, to garnish

1 Place the pork, prawns, garlic, spring onions, coriander, egg white, soy sauce and lemon rind in a food processor or blender and pulse until the mixture is fairly smooth.

2 Flatten the bread slices with a rolling pin, then spread about 5mm/¼in of the pork and prawn mixture on each slice, pressing down well. Cut each slice of bread into four triangles.

3 Sprinkle the sesame seeds in a shallow bowl and coat the triangles meat-side down with the seeds.

4 Heat 1cm/½in oil in a frying pan until a cube of bread browns in 30 seconds. Fry the toasts meat side down for 3–4 minutes, then turn them over and fry for 2 minutes. Drain on kitchen paper and serve hot, with lemon wedges, and coriander, to garnish.

MEDITERRANEAN GARLIC TOAST

Mediterranean garlic toast, or *bruschetta*, is served as an appetizer in Spain, Greece and Italy. With a topping of plum tomatoes, mozzarella cheese and salami, it makes a filling snack.

INGREDIENTS

Serves 4
150g/5oz mozzarella cheese, drained
2 plum tomatoes
½ French loaf
1 garlic clove, halved
30ml/2 tbsp olive oil, plus extra for
   brushing
12 small salami slices
15ml/1 tbsp fresh torn basil, or 5ml/
   1 tsp dried basil
salt and black pepper
fresh basil sprigs, to garnish

1 Preheat the grill to a medium heat. Cut the mozzarella cheese into twelve slices and each tomato into six slices. Cut the French bread in half and slice each half horizontally.

2 Place the bread under the grill, cut side up, and toast lightly. While the bread is still warm, rub the cut sides of the garlic clove on each cut side of the bread, then drizzle over about 7.5ml/ ½ tbsp of the olive oil.

3 Top each toast with three slices of tomato, three slices of mozzarella and three slices of salami. Brush the tops with a little more olive oil, season well and sprinkle over the basil.

4 Return to the grill and toast for 2–3 minutes, until the cheese has melted. Remove and serve hot, garnished with sprigs of fresh basil.

ENGLISH PLOUGHMAN'S PÂTÉ

────── INGREDIENTS ──────

Serves 4

50g/2oz/3 tbsp full fat soft cheese
50g/2oz/¼ cup grated Caerphilly cheese
50g/2oz/¼ cup grated Double
 Gloucester cheese
4 silverskin pickled onions, drained and
 finely chopped
15ml/1 tbsp apricot chutney
25g/1oz/2 tbsp butter, melted
30ml/2 tbsp snipped fresh chives
salt and black pepper
4 slices soft grain bread
watercress and cherry tomatoes,
 to serve

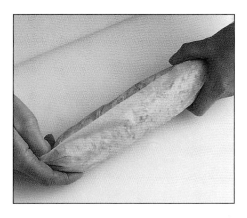

1 Mix together the soft cheese, grated cheeses, onions, chutney and butter in a bowl and season lightly.

2 Spoon the mixture on to a sheet of greaseproof paper and roll up into a cylinder, smoothing the mixture into a roll with your hands. Scrunch the ends of the paper together and twist to seal. Pop in the freezer for about 30 minutes, until just firm.

3 Spread the chives on a plate, then unwrap the chilled cheese pâté. Roll in the chives until evenly coated. Wrap in clear film and chill for 10 minutes.

4 Preheat the grill. Toast the bread lightly on both sides. Cut off the crusts and slice each piece in half horizontally. Cut each half into two triangles. Grill, untoasted side up, until golden and curled at the edges.

5 Slice the pâté into rounds and serve three or four rounds per person with the Melba toast, watercress and cherry tomatoes.

GOLDEN CHEESE PUFFS

Serve these deep-fried puffs –
called *aigrettes* in France – with
a fruity chutney and salad.

INGREDIENTS

Makes 8

50g/2oz/½ cup plain flour
15g/½oz/1 tbsp butter
1 egg plus 1 egg yolk
50g/2oz/1 cup finely grated mature
 Cheddar cheese
15ml/1 tbsp grated Parmesan cheese
2.5ml/½ tsp mustard powder
pinch of cayenne pepper
oil, for frying
salt and black pepper

1 Sift the flour on to a square of
greaseproof paper and set aside.
Place the butter and 150ml/¼ pint/
⅔ cup water in a pan and heat gently
until the butter has melted.

2 Bring the liquid to the boil and tip
in the flour all at once. Remove
from the heat and stir well with a
wooden spoon until the mixture begins
to leave the sides of the pan and forms
a ball. Allow to cool slightly.

3 Beat the egg and egg yolk together
in a bowl with a fork and then gradually add to the mixture in the pan,
beating well after each addition.

4 Stir the cheeses, mustard powder
and cayenne pepper into the
mixture and season well.

5 Heat the oil in a pan to 190°C/
375°F or until a cube of bread
browns in 30 seconds. Drop four
spoonfuls of the cheese mixture into
the oil at a time and deep-fry for 2–3
minutes until golden. Drain on kitchen
paper and keep hot in the oven while
cooking the remaining mixture. Serve
two puffs per person with a spoonful of
mango chutney and green salad.

FRENCH GOAT'S CHEESE SALAD

INGREDIENTS

Serves 4
200g/7oz bag prepared mixed salad leaves
4 rashers back bacon
16 thin slices French bread
115g/4oz full fat goat's cheese

For the dressing
60ml/4 tbsp olive oil
15ml/1 tbsp tarragon vinegar
10ml/2 tsp walnut oil
5ml/1 tsp Dijon mustard
5ml/1 tsp wholegrain mustard

1 Preheat the grill to a medium heat. Rinse and dry the salad leaves, then arrange in four individual bowls. Place the ingredients for the dressing in a screw-topped jar, shake together well and reserve.

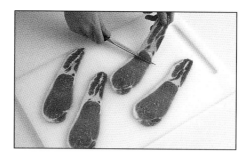

2 Lay the bacon rashers on a board, then stretch with the back of a knife and cut each into four. Roll each piece up and grill for about 2–3 minutes.

3 Meanwhile, slice the goat's cheese into eight and halve each slice. Top each slice of bread with a piece of goat's cheese and pop under the grill. Turn over the bacon and continue cooking with the goat's cheese toasts until the cheese is golden and bubbling.

4 Arrange the bacon rolls and toasts on top of the prepared salad leaves, shake the dressing well and pour a little of the dressing over each one.

> COOK'S TIP
> If you prefer, just slice the goat's cheese and place on toasted French bread. Or use wholewheat toast for a delicious nutty flavour.

GREEK SALAD PITTAS

Horiatiki is the Greek name for this classic salad made with Feta – a cheese made from ewes' milk. Try serving it in hot pitta breads with a minty yogurt dressing.

INGREDIENTS

Makes 4
115g/4oz/1 cup diced Feta cheese
¼ cucumber, peeled and diced
8 cherry tomatoes, quartered
½ small green pepper, seeded and thinly sliced
¼ small onion, thinly sliced
8 black olives, stoned and halved
30ml/2 tbsp olive oil
5ml/1 tsp dried oregano
4 large pitta breads
60ml/4 tbsp natural yogurt
5ml/1 tsp dried mint
salt and black pepper
fresh mint, to garnish

1 Place the cheese, cucumber, tomatoes, pepper, onion and olives in a bowl. Stir in the olive oil and oregano, then season well and reserve.

2 Place the pitta breads in a toaster or under a preheated grill for about 2 minutes, until puffed up. Meanwhile, to make the dressing, mix the yogurt with the mint, season well and reserve.

3 Holding the hot pittas in a dish towel, slice each one from top to bottom down one of the longest sides and open out to form a pocket.

4 Divide the prepared salad among the pitta breads and drizzle over a spoonful of the dressing. Serve the pittas immediately, garnished with the fresh mint.

KANSAS CITY FRITTERS

Makes 8

*200g/7oz/1¼ cups canned sweetcorn,
  drained well*
2 eggs, separated
90ml/6 tbsp plain flour
75ml/5 tbsp milk
1 small courgette, grated
2 rashers rindless back bacon, diced
2 spring onions, finely chopped
a good pinch of cayenne pepper
45ml/3 tbsp sunflower oil
salt and black pepper
fresh coriander sprigs, to garnish

For the salsa

3 tomatoes, skinned, seeded and diced
½ small red pepper, seeded and diced
½ small onion, diced
15ml/1 tbsp lemon juice
15ml/1 tbsp chopped fresh coriander
dash of Tabasco sauce
salt and black pepper

1 To make the salsa, place all the ingredients in a bowl, mix well and season. Cover and chill.

2 Empty the sweetcorn into a bowl and mix in the egg yolks. Add the flour and blend in with a wooden spoon. When the mixture thickens, gradually blend in the milk.

3 Stir in the courgette, bacon, spring onions, cayenne pepper and seasoning and set aside.

4 Place the egg whites in a clean bowl and whisk until stiff. Gently fold into the sweetcorn batter mixture with a metal spoon.

5 Heat 30ml/2 tbsp of the oil in a large frying pan and place four large spoonfuls of the mixture into the oil. Fry on a moderate heat for 2–3 minutes on each side until golden, then drain on kitchen paper. Keep warm in the oven while frying the remaining four fritters, adding 15ml/1 tbsp oil if necessary.

6 Serve two fritters each, garnished with coriander sprigs and a spoonful of the chilled tomato salsa.

TEX-MEX BAKED POTATOES WITH CHILLI

INGREDIENTS

Serves 4

2 large potatoes
15ml/1 tbsp oil
1 garlic clove, crushed
1 small onion, chopped
½ small red pepper, seeded and chopped
225g/8oz lean minced beef
½ small fresh red chilli, seeded and
    chopped
5ml/1 tsp ground cumin
pinch of cayenne pepper
200g/7oz can chopped tomatoes
30ml/2 tbsp tomato purée
2.5ml/½ tsp dried oregano
2.5ml/½ tsp dried marjoram
200g/7oz can red kidney beans, drained
15ml/1 tbsp chopped fresh coriander
salt and black pepper
60ml/4 tbsp soured cream
chopped fresh parsley, to garnish

1 Preheat the oven to 220°C/425°F/ Gas 7. Rub the potatoes with a little oil and pierce with skewers. Bake them on the top shelf for 30 minutes before beginning to cook the chilli.

2 Heat the oil in a pan and add the garlic, onion and pepper. Fry gently for 4–5 minutes, until softened.

3 Add the beef and fry until browned all over, then stir in the chilli, cumin, cayenne pepper, tomatoes, tomato purée, 60ml/4 tbsp water and the herbs. Cover and simmer for about 25 minutes, stirring occasionally.

4 Remove the lid, stir in the kidney beans and cook for 5 minutes. Turn off the heat and stir in the chopped coriander. Season well and set aside.

5 Cut the baked potatoes in half and place them in serving bowls. Top with the chilli mixture and a dollop of soured cream and garnish with chopped fresh parsley.

SCRAMBLED EGG AND SALMON MUFFINS

A traditional British breakfast dish – delicious when piled high on top of a hot toasted wholemeal muffin.

─── INGREDIENTS ───

Serves 4

4 eggs
45ml/3 tbsp single cream or top of the milk
4 wholemeal muffins
25g/1oz/2 tbsp butter, plus extra for spreading
15ml/1 tbsp snipped chives
2.5ml/½ tsp grated lemon rind
115g/4oz smoked salmon or trout, snipped into strips
salt and black pepper
snipped chives, to garnish

1 Break the eggs into a bowl, pour on the cream or milk and season well. Beat lightly with a fork.

2 Halve the muffins and grill until lightly toasted on both sides. Spread with a little butter and keep warm.

3 Meanwhile, melt the butter in a saucepan over a gentle heat, add the eggs and stir occasionally with a wooden spoon until just beginning to set.

4 Add the chives, lemon rind and smoked salmon or trout and stir until just set but still moist. Spoon on to the toasted muffins and garnish with snipped chives. Serve at once.

COOK'S TIP
Don't overcook the scrambled eggs – remove the pan from the heat while they are still quite creamy.

SPANISH OMELETTE

A traditional Spanish omelette consists of potato, onion and egg and is served as *tapas* or bar food. With mixed peppers and spicy sausage, it makes a filling lunchtime snack.

─── INGREDIENTS ───

Serves 4

60ml/4 tbsp olive oil
1 small onion, thinly sliced
1 small red pepper, seeded and sliced
1 small yellow pepper, seeded and sliced
1 large potato, peeled, boiled and diced
115g/4oz/1 cup sliced Chorizo sausage
4 eggs
salt and black pepper
chopped fresh parsley, to garnish

1 Heat 30ml/2 tbsp of the oil in a frying pan, add the onion and peppers and cook for 7 minutes, stirring occasionally until softened.

2 Add the remaining oil, potatoes and sausage and cook for a further 3–4 minutes. Reduce the heat slightly.

3 Place the eggs in a bowl, season well and beat lightly with a fork. Pour the eggs over the vegetable and sausage mixture and shake the pan gently.

4 Cook gently for about 5–6 minutes, until beginning to set. Place an upturned plate on top of the pan and carefully turn the omelette upside-down on to the plate.

5 Slide the omelette back into the pan and continue cooking for a further 3 minutes, until the centre is just set but still moist. Sprinkle with parsley, cut into wedges and serve straight from the pan.

FRENCH FRIED FISH GOUJONS

INGREDIENTS

Serves 4

60ml/4 tbsp mayonnaise
30ml/2 tbsp natural yogurt
grated rind of ½ lemon
squeeze of lemon juice
15ml/1 tbsp chopped fresh parsley
15ml/1 tbsp capers, chopped
2 x 175g/6oz sole fillets, skinned
2 x 175g/6oz plaice fillets, skinned
1 egg, lightly beaten
115g/4oz/2 cups fresh white bread-
    crumbs
15ml/1 tbsp sesame seeds
pinch of paprika
salt and black pepper
oil, for frying
4 lemon wedges, to serve
watercress, to garnish

1 To make the lemon mayonnaise, mix together the mayonnaise, yogurt, lemon rind and juice, parsley and capers in a bowl. Cover and chill.

2 Cut the fish fillets into thin strips. Place the beaten egg in one shallow bowl. In another bowl, mix together the breadcrumbs, sesame seeds, paprika and seasoning.

3 Dip the fish strips, one at a time, into the beaten egg, then into the breadcrumb mixture and toss until coated evenly. Lay on a clean plate.

4 Heat about 2.5cm/1in of oil in a frying pan until a cube of bread browns in 30 seconds. Deep-fry the strips in batches for 2–3 minutes, until lightly golden.

5 Remove with a slotted spoon, drain on kitchen paper and keep warm in the oven while frying the remainder. Garnish with watercress and serve hot with lemon wedges and the chilled lemon mayonnaise.

COOK'S TIP
Use any white fish fillets for the goujons – just be sure to cut them into thin strips. You could try a mixture of haddock and cod as an alternative to the sole and plaice.

GARLIC CHILLI PRAWNS

In Spain *Gambas al Ajillo* are traditionally cooked in small earthenware dishes, but a frying pan is just as good.

INGREDIENTS

Serves 4

60ml/4 tbsp olive oil
2–3 garlic cloves, finely chopped
½–1 fresh red chilli, seeded and chopped
16 cooked whole Mediterranean
    prawns
15ml/1 tbsp chopped fresh parsley
salt and black pepper
lemon wedges and French bread,
    to serve

1 Heat the oil in a large frying pan and add the garlic and chilli. Stir-fry for 1 minute, until the garlic begins to turn brown.

2 Add the Mediterranean prawns and stir-fry for 3–4 minutes, coating them well with the flavoured oil.

3 Add the parsley, remove from the heat and serve four prawns per person in heated bowls, with the flavoured oil spooned over them. Serve with lemon wedges for squeezing and French bread to mop up the juices.

MEAT DISHES

This chapter is full of hearty meat-based, main meal dishes, from special-occasion centrepieces to more informal family fare. They range from Mexican Spiced Roast Leg of Lamb spiked with garlic, herbs and spices for an unusual Sunday roast, to a favourite South African dish – Spiced Lamb Bake, a delicious alternative shepherd's pie with a light golden, creamy coconut and egg custard topping. Not forgetting all-time favourites like Best-ever American Burgers, Corned Beef and Egg Hash, a hearty Breton Pork and Bean Casserole, Hungarian Beef Goulash with herby dumplings, and a truly scrumptious Bacon and Sausage Sauerkraut from Alsace.

BRETON PORK AND BEAN CASSEROLE

INGREDIENTS

Serves 4

30ml/2 tbsp olive oil
1 onion, chopped
2 garlic cloves, chopped
450g/1lb lean shoulder of pork, cubed
340g/12oz lean lamb (preferably leg), cubed
225g/8oz coarse pork and garlic sausage, cut into chunks
400g/14oz can chopped tomatoes
30ml/2 tbsp red wine
15ml/1 tbsp tomato purée
bouquet garni
400g/14oz can cannellini beans, drained
50g/2oz/1 cup brown breadcrumbs
salt and black pepper
salad and French bread, to serve

1 Preheat the oven to 160°C/325°F/ Gas 3. Heat the oil in a large flameproof casserole and fry the onions and garlic until softened. Remove with a draining spoon and reserve.

2 Add the pork, lamb and sausage to the pan and fry on a high heat until browned on all sides. Return the onions and garlic to the pan.

3 Stir in the chopped tomatoes, wine and tomato purée and add 300ml/ ½pint/1¼ cups water. Season well and pop in the bouquet garni.

4 Cover and bring to the boil, then transfer the casserole to the preheated oven and cook for 1½ hours.

5 Remove the bouquet garni, stir in the beans and sprinkle the breadcrumbs over the top. Return to the oven, uncovered, for a further 30 minutes, until the top is golden brown. Serve hot with a green salad and French bread to mop up the juices.

> COOK'S TIP
> Replace the lamb with duck breast, if you like, but be sure to drain off any fat before sprinkling with the breadcrumbs.

CHEESY PASTA BOLOGNESE

Serves 4

30ml/2 tbsp olive oil
1 onion, chopped
1 garlic clove, crushed
1 carrot, diced
2 celery sticks, chopped
2 rashers streaky bacon, finely chopped
5 button mushrooms, chopped
450g/1lb lean minced beef
120ml/4fl oz/½ cup red wine
15ml/1 tbsp tomato purée
200g/7oz can chopped tomatoes
sprig of fresh thyme
225g/8oz/2 cups dried penne pasta
300ml/½ pint/1¼ cups milk
25g/1oz/2 tbsp butter
25g/1oz/2 tbsp plain flour
150g/5oz/1 cup cubed mozzarella
  cheese
60ml/4 tbsp grated Parmesan cheese
salt and black pepper
fresh basil sprigs, to garnish

1 Heat the oil in a pan and fry the onion, garlic, carrot and celery for 6 minutes, until the onions have softened.

2 Add the bacon and continue frying for 3–4 minutes. Stir in the mushrooms, fry for 2 minutes, then add the beef. Fry on a high heat until well browned all over.

3 Pour in the red wine, the tomato purée dissolved in 45ml/3 tbsp water, and the tomatoes, then add the thyme and season well. Bring to the boil, cover the pan and simmer gently for about 30 minutes.

4 Preheat the oven to 200°C/400°F/ Gas 6. Bring a pan of water to the boil, add a little oil and cook the pasta for 10 minutes.

5 Meanwhile, place the milk, butter and flour in a saucepan, heat gently and whisk continuously with a balloon whisk until thickened. Stir in the mozzarella cheese, 30ml/2 tbsp of the Parmesan and season lightly.

6 Drain the pasta when it is ready and stir into the cheese sauce. Uncover the Bolognese sauce and boil rapidly for 2 minutes to reduce the liquid.

7 Spoon the sauce into an ovenproof dish, top with the pasta mixture and sprinkle the remaining 30ml/2 tbsp Parmesan cheese evenly over the top. Bake for 25 minutes until golden. Garnish with basil and serve hot.

BEST-EVER AMERICAN BURGERS

INGREDIENTS

Makes 4 burgers

15ml/1 tbsp vegetable oil
1 small onion, finely chopped
450g/1lb minced beef
1 large garlic clove, crushed
5ml/1 tsp ground cumin
10ml/2 tsp ground coriander
30ml/2 tbsp tomato purée or ketchup
5ml/1 tsp wholegrain mustard
dash of Worcestershire sauce
30ml/2 tbsp chopped fresh mixed herbs
*   (parsley, thyme and oregano or*
*   marjoram)*
15ml/1 tbsp lightly beaten egg
salt and black pepper
flour, for shaping
oil, for frying (optional)
mixed salad, chips and relish, to serve

1 Heat the oil in a frying pan, add the onion and cook for 5 minutes, until softened. Remove from the pan, drain on kitchen paper and leave to cool.

2 Mix together the beef, garlic, spices, tomato purée or ketchup, mustard, Worcestershire sauce, herbs, beaten egg and seasoning in a bowl. Stir in the cooled onions.

3 Sprinkle a board with flour and shape the mixture into four burgers with floured hands and a palette knife. Cover and chill for 15 minutes.

4 Heat a little oil in a pan and fry the burgers on a medium heat for about 5 minutes each side, depending on how rare you like them. Alternatively, cook under a medium grill for the same time. Serve with salad, chips and relish.

BACON AND SAUSAGE SAUERKRAUT

Juniper and coriander flavour this traditional dish from Alsace.

INGREDIENTS

Serves 4

30ml/2 tbsp oil
1 large onion, thinly sliced
1 garlic clove, crushed
450g/1lb bottled sauerkraut, rinsed and
*   drained*
1 eating apple, cored and chopped
5 juniper berries
5 coriander seeds, crushed
450g/1lb piece of lightly smoked bacon
*   loin roast*
225g/8oz whole smoked pork sausage,
*   pricked*
175ml/6fl oz/¾ cup unsweetened apple
*   juice*
150ml/¼ pint/⅔ cup chicken stock
1 bay leaf
8 small salad potatoes

1 Preheat the oven to 180°C/350°F/ Gas 4. Heat the oil in a flameproof casserole and fry the onion and garlic for 3–4 minutes, until softened. Stir in the sauerkraut, apple, juniper berries and coriander seeds.

2 Lay the piece of bacon and sausage on top of the sauerkraut, pour on the apple juice and stock and add the bay leaf. Cover and bake in the oven for about 1 hour.

3 Remove from the oven and pop the potatoes into the casserole. Add a little more stock if necessary, cover and bake for a further 30 minutes, or until the potatoes are tender.

4 Just before serving, lift out the bacon and sausages on to a board and slice. Spoon the sauerkraut on to a warmed platter, top with the meat and surround with the potatoes.

CORNED BEEF AND EGG HASH

This classic American hash is made with corned beef and is a popular brunch or lunchtime dish all over the United States. Serve with chilli sauce for a really authentic touch.

INGREDIENTS

Serves 4

30ml/2 tbsp vegetable oil
25g/1oz/2 tbsp butter
1 onion, finely chopped
1 small green pepper, seeded and diced
2 large boiled potatoes, diced
350g/12oz can corned beef, cubed
1.25ml/¼ tsp grated nutmeg
1.25ml/¼ tsp paprika
4 eggs
salt and black pepper
chopped fresh parsley, to garnish
sweet chilli sauce or tomato sauce, to serve

1 Heat the oil and butter together in a large frying pan and add the onion. Fry for 5–6 minutes, until softened.

2 In a bowl, mix together the pepper, potatoes, corned beef, nutmeg and paprika and season well. Add to the pan and toss gently to distribute the cooked onion. Press down lightly and fry on a medium heat for about 3–4 minutes, until a golden brown crust has formed on the bottom.

3 Stir the mixture through to distribute the crust, then repeat the frying twice, until the mixture is well browned.

4 Make four wells in the hash and crack an egg into each one. Cover and cook gently for about 4–5 minutes, until the egg whites are just set.

5 Sprinkle with chopped parsley and cut the hash into quarters. Serve hot with sweet chilli sauce.

> **COOK'S TIP**
> Pop the can of corned beef into the fridge to chill for about half an hour before using – it will firm up and cut into cubes more easily.

HUNGARIAN BEEF GOULASH

Serves 4

30ml/2 tbsp vegetable oil
1kg/2lb braising steak, cubed
2 onions, chopped
1 garlic clove, crushed
15ml/1 tbsp plain flour
10ml/2 tsp paprika
5ml/1 tsp caraway seeds
400g/14oz can chopped tomatoes
300ml/½ pint/1¼ cups beef stock
1 large carrot, chopped
1 red pepper, seeded and chopped
soured cream, to serve
pinch of paprika, to garnish

For the dumplings

115g/4oz/1 cup self-raising flour
50g/2oz/½ cup shredded suet
15ml/1 tbsp chopped fresh parsley
2.5ml/½ tsp caraway seeds
salt and black pepper

1 Heat the oil in a flameproof casserole, add the meat and fry over a high heat for 5 minutes, stirring, until browned. Remove with a slotted spoon.

2 Add the onions and garlic and fry gently for 5 minutes, until softened. Add the flour, paprika and caraway seeds, stir and cook for 2 minutes.

3 Return the browned meat to the casserole and stir in the tomatoes and stock. Bring to the boil, cover and simmer gently for 2 hours.

4 Meanwhile, make the dumplings. Sift the flour and seasoning into a bowl, add the suet, parsley, caraway seeds and about 45–60ml/3–4 tbsp water and mix to a soft dough. Divide into eight pieces and roll into balls. Cover and reserve.

5 After 2 hours, stir the carrot and pepper into the goulash and season well. Drop the dumplings into the goulash, cover and simmer for about 25 minutes. Serve in bowls topped with a spoonful of soured cream sprinkled with a pinch of paprika.

PEKING BEEF AND PEPPER STIR-FRY

INGREDIENTS

Serves 4

350g/12oz rump or sirloin steak, sliced
    into strips
30ml/2 tbsp soy sauce
30ml/2 tbsp medium sherry
15ml/1 tbsp cornflour
5ml/1 tsp brown sugar
15ml/1 tbsp sunflower oil
15ml/1 tbsp sesame oil
1 garlic clove, finely chopped
15ml/1 tbsp grated fresh root ginger
1 red pepper, seeded and sliced
1 yellow pepper, seeded and sliced
115g/4oz sugar snap peas
4 spring onions, cut into 5cm/2in
    pieces
30ml/2 tbsp Chinese oyster sauce
hot noodles, to serve

1 In a bowl, mix together the steak strips, soy sauce, sherry, cornflour and brown sugar. Cover and leave to marinate for 30 minutes.

2 Heat the oils in a wok or large frying pan. Add the garlic and ginger and stir-fry quickly for about 30 seconds. Add the peppers, sugar snap peas and spring onions and stir-fry over a high heat for 3 minutes.

3 Add the beef with the marinade juices to the wok or frying pan and stir-fry for a further 3–4 minutes.

4 Finally, pour in the oyster sauce and 60ml/4 tbsp water and stir until the sauce has thickened slightly. Serve immediately with hot noodles.

TEXAN BARBECUED RIBS

An American favourite of pork spare ribs cooked in a sweet and sour barbecue sauce. Ideal as a barbecue dish, this can be just as easily cooked in the oven.

INGREDIENTS

Serves 4

1.5kg/3lb (about 16) lean pork spare
    ribs
1 onion, finely chopped
1 large garlic clove, crushed
120ml/4fl oz/½ cup tomato ketchup
30ml/2 tbsp orange juice
30ml/2 tbsp red wine vinegar
5ml/1 tsp mustard
10ml/2 tsp clear honey
30ml/2 tbsp soft light brown sugar
dash of Worcestershire sauce
30ml/2 tbsp vegetable oil
salt and black pepper
chopped fresh parsley, to garnish

1 Preheat the oven to 200°C/400°F/ Gas 6. Place the pork spare ribs in a large shallow roasting tin and bake for 20 minutes.

2 Meanwhile, mix together in a saucepan the onion, garlic, tomato ketchup, orange juice, wine vinegar, mustard, clear honey, brown sugar, Worcestershire sauce, oil and seasoning. Bring to the boil and simmer for about 5 minutes.

3 Remove the ribs from the oven and reduce the temperature to 180°C/ 350°F/Gas 4. Spoon over half the sauce, covering the ribs well and bake for 20 minutes. Turn them over, baste with the remaining sauce and cook for a further 25 minutes.

4 Sprinkle the ribs with parsley and serve three or four ribs per person. Provide small finger bowls for washing sticky fingers.

TURKISH LAMB AND APRICOT STEW

INGREDIENTS

Serves 4

1 large aubergine, cubed
30ml/2 tbsp sunflower oil
1 onion, chopped
1 garlic clove, crushed
5ml/1 tsp ground cinnamon
3 whole cloves
450g/1lb boned leg of lamb, cubed
400g/14oz can chopped tomatoes
115g/4oz/⅔ cup ready-to-eat dried
  apricots
115g/4oz canned chick-peas, drained
5ml/1 tsp clear honey
salt and black pepper
couscous, to serve
30ml/2 tbsp olive oil
30ml/2 tbsp chopped almonds, fried in
  a little oil
chopped fresh parsley

1 Place the aubergine in a colander, sprinkle with salt and leave for 30 minutes. Heat the oil in a flameproof casserole, add the onions and garlic and fry for 5 minutes, until softened.

2 Stir in the ground cinnamon and cloves and fry for 1 minute. Add the lamb and cook for 5–6 minutes, stirring occasionally until well browned.

3 Rinse, drain and pat dry the aubergine, add to the pan and cook for 3 minutes, stirring well. Add the tomatoes, 300ml/½ pint/1¼ cups water, apricots and seasoning. Bring to the boil, then cover and simmer gently for about 45 minutes.

4 Stir in the chick-peas and honey and cook for a further 15–20 minutes, or until the lamb is tender. Serve the stew accompanied by couscous with the olive oil, fried almonds and chopped parsley stirred in.

THAI PORK SATAY WITH PEANUT SAUCE

INGREDIENTS

Makes 8

½ small onion, finely chopped
2 garlic cloves, crushed
30ml/2 tbsp lemon juice
15ml/1 tbsp soy sauce
5ml/1 tsp ground coriander
2.5ml/½ tsp ground cumin
5ml/1 tsp ground turmeric
30ml/2 tbsp vegetable oil
450g/1lb pork tenderloin
fresh coriander sprigs, to garnish
boiled rice, to serve

For the sauce

50g/2oz creamed coconut, chopped
60ml/4 tbsp crunchy peanut butter
15ml/1 tbsp lemon juice
2.5ml/½ tsp ground cumin
2.5ml/½ tsp ground coriander
5ml/1 tsp soft brown sugar
15ml/1 tbsp soy sauce
1–2 dried red chillies, or ½ fresh red
    chilli, seeded and finely chopped
15ml/1 tbsp chopped fresh coriander
    (leaves and stems)

For the salad

½ small cucumber, peeled and diced
15ml/1 tbsp white wine vinegar
15ml/1 tbsp chopped fresh coriander
salt and black pepper

1 Soak eight wooden skewers in water
for about 30 minutes – this will prevent them charring during grilling.

2 Place the onion, garlic, lemon juice,
soy sauce, ground spices and oil
into a food processor or blender and
pulse until smooth, or mix in a bowl.

3 Cut the pork into thin strips and
place in a bowl, spoon over the
marinade and mix well. Cover and chill
for at least 2 hours.

4 Preheat the grill to the hottest set-
ting. Thread about two or three
pieces of pork on to each skewer and
grill on a rack for 2–3 minutes each
side, basting once with the marinade.

5 Meanwhile, make the sauce.
Dissolve the creamed coconut in
150ml/¼ pint/⅔ cup of boiling water.
Put the remaining ingredients into a
pan and stir in the coconut liquid. Bring
to the boil, stirring well and simmer
gently for 5 minutes, until thick.

6 Mix together the salad ingredients.
Arrange the satay sticks on a platter
and garnish with coriander sprigs. Serve
with bowls of sauce, salad and rice.

MIDDLE EASTERN LAMB KEBABS

Skewered, grilled meats are the main item in many Middle Eastern and Greek restaurants. In this recipe marinated lamb is grilled with vegetables.

─────── INGREDIENTS ───────

Makes 4
450g/1lb boneless leg of lamb, cubed
75ml/5 tbsp olive oil
15ml/1 tbsp chopped fresh oregano or
    thyme, or 10ml/2 tsp dried oregano
15ml/1 tbsp chopped fresh parsley
juice of ½ lemon
½ small aubergine, thickly sliced and
    quartered
4 baby onions, halved
2 tomatoes, quartered
4 fresh bay leaves
salt and black pepper
pitta bread and natural yogurt,
    to serve

1 Place the lamb in a bowl. Mix together the olive oil, oregano, parsley, lemon juice and seasoning, pour over the lamb and mix well. Cover and marinate for about 1 hour.

2 Preheat the grill. Thread the marinated lamb, aubergine, onions, tomatoes and bay leaves alternately on to four large skewers.

3 Place the kebabs on a grill rack and brush the vegetables liberally with the leftover marinade. Cook the kebabs under a medium heat for about 8–10 minutes on each side, basting once or twice with the juices that have collected in the bottom of the grill pan. Serve the kebabs hot, with hot pitta bread and natural yogurt.

COOK'S TIP
Make a lemony bulgur wheat salad to accompany the kebabs if you like. Or serve them with plain, boiled rice – either basmati or jasmine rice would be a good choice.

MEXICAN SPICED ROAST LEG OF LAMB

─────── INGREDIENTS ───────

Serves 4
1 small leg or half leg of lamb (about
    1.25kg/2½lb)
15ml/1 tbsp dried oregano
5ml/1 tsp ground cumin
5ml/1 tsp hot chilli powder
2 garlic cloves
45ml/3 tbsp olive oil
30ml/2 tbsp red wine vinegar
salt and black pepper
fresh oregano sprigs, to garnish

1 Preheat the oven to 220°C/425°F/Gas 7. Place the leg of lamb on a large chopping board.

2 Place the oregano, cumin, chilli powder and one of the garlic cloves, crushed, into a bowl. Pour on half of the olive oil and mix well to form a paste. Set the paste aside.

3 Using a sharp knife, make a criss-cross pattern of fairly deep slits through the skin and just into the meat.

4 Press the spice paste into the meat slits with the back of a knife.

5 Slice the remaining garlic clove thinly and cut each slice in half again. Push the pieces of garlic deeply into the slits in the meat (to prevent burning during roasting).

6 Mix the vinegar and remaining oil, pour over the joint and season with salt and freshly ground black pepper.

7 Bake for about 15 minutes at the higher temperature, then reduce the heat to 180°C/350°F/Gas 4 and cook for a further 1¼ hours (or a little longer if you like your meat well done). Serve the lamb with a delicious gravy made with the spicy pan juices and garnish with fresh oregano sprigs.

BOEUF BOURGUIGNON

This French classic is named after the region it comes from, Burgundy, where the local red wine is used to flavour this delicious stew.

INGREDIENTS

Serves 4

30ml/2 tbsp olive oil
225g/8oz piece streaky bacon, cubed
12 whole baby onions
1kg/2lb braising steak, cut into
  5cm/2in squares
1 large onion, sliced
15ml/1 tbsp plain flour
about 450ml/¾ pint red Burgundy wine
bouquet garni
1 garlic clove
225g/8oz button mushrooms, halved
salt and black pepper
chopped fresh parsley, to garnish

1 Heat the oil in a flameproof casserole and add the bacon and baby onions. Fry for 7–8 minutes, until the onions have browned and the bacon fat is transparent. Remove with a slotted spoon and reserve.

2 Add the beef to the pan and fry quickly on all sides until browned. Add the sliced onion and continue cooking for 4–5 minutes.

3 Sprinkle over the flour and stir well. Pour over the wine and add the bouquet garni and garlic. Cover and simmer gently for about 2 hours. Stir in the reserved sautéed onions and bacon and add a little extra wine, if necessary.

4 Add the mushrooms. Cover and cook for a further 30 minutes. Remove the bouquet garni and garlic and garnish with chopped fresh parsley.

SPICED LAMB BAKE

A quite delicious South African shepherd's pie. The recipe was originally poached from the Afrikaners' Malay slaves, hence the slightly oriental flavour.

INGREDIENTS

Serves 4

15ml/1 tbsp vegetable oil
1 medium onion, chopped
675g/1½lb minced lamb
30ml/2 tbsp medium curry paste
30ml/2 tbsp mango chutney
30ml/2 tbsp lemon juice
60ml/4 tbsp chopped, blanched
  almonds
30ml/2 tbsp sultanas
75g/3oz creamed coconut, crumbled
2 eggs
2 bay leaves
salt and black pepper

1 Preheat the oven to 180°C/350°F/ Gas 4.

2 Heat the oil in a frying pan, add the onion and cook for about 5–6 minutes, until softened.

3 Add the lamb and cook on a medium heat, turning frequently until browned all over. Stir in the curry paste, chutney, lemon juice, almonds and sultanas, season well and cook for about 5 minutes.

4 Transfer the mixture to an oven-proof dish and cook in the oven, uncovered, for 10 minutes.

5 Meanwhile, dissolve the creamed coconut in 200ml/7fl oz/⅞ cup boiling water and cool slightly. Beat in the eggs and a little seasoning.

6 Remove the dish from the oven and pour the coconut custard over the meat mixture. Lay the bay leaves on the top and return the dish to the oven for 30–35 minutes, or until the top is set and golden. Serve hot.

POULTRY AND GAME

Chicken, turkey and game are favourite ingredients in most households and this chapter combines popular classics such as a rich and warming Coq au Vin from Burgundy, and the simple but delicious Normandy Roast Chicken, with some more exotic delights that you will want to cook over and over again. From the heart of Louisiana comes the ultimate chicken 'n' rice dish, Chicken Jambalaya, a great family meal-in-one, and from India comes a Chicken Biryani that will outshine any take-away version. The Country Cider Hot-Pot, studded with succulent prunes, is a great British winter warmer, and the simple pan-fried Crumbed Turkey Steaks, with their crunchy coating and a squeeze of lemon juice, will appeal to all members of the family.

FRENCH-STYLE POT-ROAST POUSSIN

INGREDIENTS

Serves 4

15ml/1 tbsp olive oil
1 onion, sliced
1 large garlic clove, sliced
50g/2oz/½ cup diced lightly smoked
    bacon
2 fresh poussin (just under 450g/1lb
    each)
30ml/2 tbsp melted butter
2 baby celery hearts, each cut into 4
8 baby carrots
2 small courgettes, cut into chunks
8 small new potatoes
600ml/1 pint/2½ cups chicken stock
150ml/¼ pint/⅔ cup dry white wine
1 bay leaf
2 fresh thyme sprigs
2 fresh rosemary sprigs
15ml/1 tbsp butter, softened
15ml/1 tbsp plain flour
salt and black pepper
fresh herbs, to garnish

1 Preheat the oven to 190°C/375°F/
Gas 5. Heat the olive oil in a large
flameproof casserole and add the
onion, garlic and bacon. Sauté for 5–6
minutes, until the onions have softened.

2 Brush the poussin with a little of the
melted butter and season well. Lay
on top of the onion mixture and
arrange the prepared vegetables around
them. Pour the chicken stock and wine
around the birds and add the herbs.

3 Cover, bake for 20 minutes, then
remove the lid and brush the birds
with the remaining butter. Bake for a
further 25–30 minutes until golden.

4 Transfer the poussin to a warmed
serving platter and cut each in half
with poultry shears or scissors. Remove
the vegetables with a draining spoon
and arrange them round the birds.
Cover with foil and keep warm.

5 Discard the herbs from the pan
juices. In a bowl mix together the
butter and flour to form a paste. Bring
the liquid in the pan to the boil and
then whisk in teaspoonfuls of the paste
until thickened. Season the sauce and
serve with the poussin and vegetables,
garnished with fresh herbs.

COQ AU VIN

Serves 4

45ml/3 tbsp plain flour
1.5kg/3lb chicken, cut into 8 joints
15ml/1 tbsp olive oil
50g/2oz/4 tbsp butter
20 baby onions
75g/3oz piece streaky bacon without
  rind, diced
about 20 button mushrooms
30ml/2 tbsp brandy
75cl bottle red Burgundy wine
bouquet garni
3 garlic cloves
5ml/1 tsp soft light brown sugar
15ml/1 tbsp butter, softened
15ml/1 tbsp plain flour
salt and black pepper
15ml/1 tbsp chopped fresh parsley and
  croûtons, to garnish

1 Place the flour and seasoning in a large plastic bag and shake each chicken joint in it until lightly coated. Heat the oil and butter in a large flame-proof casserole. Add the onions and bacon and sauté for 3–4 minutes, until the onions have browned lightly. Add the mushrooms and fry for 2 minutes. Remove with a slotted spoon into a bowl and reserve.

2 Add the chicken pieces to the hot oil and cook until browned on all sides, about 5–6 minutes. Pour in the brandy and (standing well back from the pan) carefully light it with a match, then shake the pan gently until the flames subside. Pour on the wine, add the bouquet garni, garlic, sugar and seasoning.

3 Bring to the boil, cover and simmer for 1 hour, stirring occasionally. Return the reserved onions, bacon and mushrooms to the casserole, cover and cook for a further 30 minutes.

4 Lift out the chicken, vegetables and bacon with a draining spoon and arrange on a warmed dish.

5 Remove the bouquet garni and boil the liquid rapidly for 2 minutes to reduce slightly. Cream the butter and flour together and whisk in teaspoonfuls of the mixture until the liquid has thickened slightly. Pour this sauce over the chicken and serve garnished with parsley and croûtons.

TANDOORI CHICKEN KEBABS

This dish originates from the plains of the Punjab at the foot of the Himalayas. There food is traditionally cooked in clay ovens known as *tandoors* – hence the name.

INGREDIENTS

Serves 4

4 boneless, skinless chicken breasts
(about 175g/6oz each)
15ml/1 tbsp lemon juice
45ml/3 tbsp tandoori paste
45ml/3 tbsp natural yogurt
1 garlic clove, crushed
30ml/2 tbsp chopped fresh coriander
1 small onion, cut into wedges and
separated into layers
a little oil, for brushing
salt and black pepper
fresh coriander sprigs, to garnish
pilau rice and naan bread, to serve

1 Chop the chicken breasts into 2.5cm/1in cubes, place in a bowl and add the lemon juice, tandoori paste, yogurt, garlic, coriander and seasoning. Cover and leave to marinate in the fridge for 2–3 hours.

2 Preheat the grill. Thread alternate pieces of marinated chicken and onion on to four skewers.

3 Brush the onions with a little oil, lay on a grill rack and cook under a high heat for 10–12 minutes, turning once. Garnish the kebabs with fresh coriander and serve at once with pilau rice and naan bread.

COOK'S TIP
Use chopped, boned and skinless chicken thighs, or turkey breasts for a cheaper alternative.

CHINESE CHICKEN WITH CASHEW NUTS

INGREDIENTS

Serves 4

4 boneless chicken breasts (about
175g/6oz each), skinned and sliced
into strips
3 garlic cloves, crushed
60ml/4 tbsp soy sauce
30ml/2 tbsp cornflour
225g/8oz dried egg noodles
45ml/3 tbsp groundnut or sunflower oil
15ml/1 tbsp sesame oil
115g/4oz/1 cup roasted cashew nuts
6 spring onions, cut into 5cm/2in pieces
and halved lengthways
spring onion curls and a little chopped
red chilli, to garnish

1 Place the chicken in a bowl with the garlic, soy sauce and cornflour and mix until the chicken is well coated. Cover and chill for about 30 minutes.

2 Meanwhile, bring a pan of water to the boil and add the egg noodles. Turn off the heat and leave to stand for 5 minutes. Drain well and reserve.

3 Heat the oils in a large frying pan or wok and add the chilled chicken and marinade juices. Stir-fry on a high heat for about 3–4 minutes, or until golden brown.

4 Add the cashew nuts and spring onions to the pan or wok and stir-fry for 2–3 minutes.

5 Add the drained noodles and stir-fry for a further 2 minutes. Toss the noodles well and serve immediately, garnished with the spring onion curls and chopped chilli.

CHINESE-STYLE CHICKEN SALAD

INGREDIENTS

Serves 4

4 boneless chicken breasts (about
   175g/6oz each)
60ml/4 tbsp dark soy sauce
pinch of Chinese five spice powder
a good squeeze of lemon juice
½ cucumber, peeled and cut into
   matchsticks
5ml/1 tsp salt
45ml/3 tbsp sunflower oil
30ml/2 tbsp sesame oil
15ml/1 tbsp sesame seeds
30ml/2 tbsp dry sherry
2 carrots, cut into matchsticks
8 spring onions, shredded
75g/3oz/1 cup beansprouts

For the sauce

60ml/4 tbsp crunchy peanut butter
10ml/2 tsp lemon juice
10ml/2 tsp sesame oil
1.25ml/¼ tsp hot chilli powder
1 spring onion, finely chopped

1 Put the chicken portions into a large pan and just cover with water. Add 15ml/1 tbsp of the soy sauce, the Chinese five spice powder and lemon juice, cover and bring to the boil, then simmer for about 20 minutes.

2 Meanwhile, place the cucumber matchsticks in a colander, sprinkle with the salt and cover with a plate with a weight on top. Leave to drain for 30 minutes – set the colander in a bowl or on a deep plate to catch the drips.

3 Lift out the poached chicken with a draining spoon and leave until cool enough to handle. Remove and discard the skins and bash the chicken lightly with a rolling pin to loosen the fibres. Slice into thin strips and reserve.

4 Heat the oils in a large frying pan or wok. Add the sesame seeds, fry for 30 seconds and then stir in the remaining 45ml/3 tbsp soy sauce and the sherry. Add the carrots and stir-fry for 2–3 minutes, until just tender. Remove from the heat and reserve.

5 Rinse the cucumber well, pat dry with kitchen paper and place in a bowl. Add the spring onions, beansprouts, cooked carrots, pan juices and shredded chicken, and mix together. Transfer to a shallow dish. Cover and chill for about 1 hour, turning the mixture in the juices once or twice.

6 To make the sauce, cream the peanut butter with the lemon juice, sesame oil and chilli powder, adding a little hot water to form a paste, then stir in the spring onion. Arrange the chicken mixture on a serving dish and serve with the peanut sauce.

CHICKEN BIRYANI

INGREDIENTS

Serves 4

275g/10oz/1½ cups basmati rice, rinsed
2.5ml/½ tsp salt
5 whole cardamom pods
2–3 whole cloves
1 cinnamon stick
45ml/3 tbsp vegetable oil
3 onions, sliced
675g/1½ lb boneless, skinned chicken
    (4 x 175g/6oz chicken breasts),
    cubed
1.25ml/¼ tsp ground cloves
5 cardamom pods, seeds removed and
    ground
1.25ml/¼ tsp hot chilli powder
5ml/1 tsp ground cumin
5ml/1 tsp ground coriander
2.5ml/½ tsp freshly ground black
    pepper
3 garlic cloves, finely chopped
5ml/1 tsp finely chopped fresh root
    ginger
juice of 1 lemon
4 tomatoes, sliced
30ml/2 tbsp chopped fresh coriander
150ml/5fl oz/⅔ cup natural yogurt
2.5ml/½ tsp saffron strands soaked in
    10ml/2 tsp hot milk
45ml/3 tbsp toasted flaked almonds
    and fresh coriander sprigs, to garnish
natural yogurt, to serve

1 Preheat the oven to 190°C/375°F/ Gas 5. Bring a pan of water to the boil and add the rice, salt, cardamom pods, cloves and cinnamon stick. Boil for 2 minutes and then drain, leaving the whole spices in the rice.

2 Heat the oil in a pan and fry the onions for 8 minutes, until browned. Add the chicken followed by all the ground spices, the garlic, ginger and lemon juice. Stir-fry for 5 minutes.

3 Transfer the chicken mixture to an ovenproof casserole and lay the tomatoes on top. Sprinkle over the fresh coriander, spoon over the yogurt and top with the drained rice.

4 Drizzle the saffron and milk over the rice and pour over 150ml/¼ pint/⅔ cup of water.

5 Cover tightly and bake in the oven for 1 hour. Transfer to a warmed serving platter and remove the whole spices from the rice. Garnish with toasted almonds and fresh coriander and serve with yogurt.

ITALIAN CHICKEN

INGREDIENTS

Serves 4
30ml/2 tbsp plain flour
4 chicken portions (legs, breasts or
    quarters)
30ml/2 tbsp olive oil
1 onion, chopped
2 garlic cloves, chopped
1 red pepper, seeded and chopped
400g/14oz can chopped tomatoes,
30ml/2 tbsp red pesto sauce
4 sun-dried tomatoes in oil, chopped
150ml/¼ pint/⅔ cup chicken stock
5ml/1 tsp dried oregano
8 black olives, stoned
salt and black pepper
chopped fresh basil and basil leaves, to
    garnish
tagliatelle, to serve

1 Place the flour and seasoning in a plastic bag. Add the chicken pieces and shake well until coated. Heat the oil in a flameproof casserole, add the chicken and brown quickly. Remove with a spoon and set aside.

2 Lower the heat and add the onion, garlic and pepper and cook for 5 minutes. Stir in the remaining ingredients, except olives and bring to the boil.

3 Return the sautéed chicken portions to the casserole, season lightly, cover and simmer for 30–35 minutes, or until the chicken is cooked.

4 Add the olives and simmer for a further 5 minutes. Transfer to a warmed serving dish, sprinkle with the chopped basil and garnish with basil leaves. Serve with hot tagliatelle.

HONEY AND ORANGE GLAZED CHICKEN

This way of cooking chicken breasts is popular in America, Australia and Great Britain. It is ideal for an easy evening meal served with baked potatoes.

INGREDIENTS

Serves 4
4 x 175g/6oz boneless chicken breasts
15ml/1 tbsp oil
4 spring onions, chopped
1 garlic clove, crushed
45ml/3 tbsp clear honey
60ml/4 tbsp fresh orange juice
1 orange, peeled and segmented
30ml/2 tbsp soy sauce
fresh lemon balm or flat leaf parsley, to
    garnish
baked potatoes and mixed salad, to
    serve

1 Preheat the oven to 190°C/375°F/ Gas 5. Place the chicken breasts in a shallow roasting tin and set aside.

2 Heat the oil in a small pan, and fry the spring onions and garlic for 2 minutes until softenend. Add the honey, orange juice, orange segments and soy sauce to the pan, stirring well until the honey has dissolved.

3 Pour over the chicken and bake, uncovered, for about 45 minutes, basting once or twice until the chicken is cooked. Garnish with lemon balm or parsley and serve the chicken and its sauce with baked potatoes and a salad.

COOK'S TIP
Look out for mustard flavoured with honey to add to this dish instead of the clear honey.

HAMPSHIRE FARMHOUSE FLAN

Serves 4

225g/8oz/2 cups wholemeal flour
50g/2oz/4 tbsp butter, cubed
50g/2oz/4 tbsp lard
5ml/1 tsp caraway seeds
15ml/1 tbsp oil
1 onion, chopped
1 garlic clove, crushed
225g/8oz/2 cups chopped cooked
   chicken
75g/3oz/2½ cups watercress leaves,
   chopped
grated rind of ½ small lemon
2 eggs, lightly beaten
175ml/6fl oz/¾ cup double cream
45ml/3 tbsp natural yogurt
a good pinch of grated nutmeg
45ml/3 tbsp grated Caerphilly cheese
beaten egg, to glaze
salt and black pepper

1 Place the flour in a bowl with a pinch of salt. Add the butter and lard and rub into the flour with your fingertips until the mixture resembles breadcrumbs. (Alternatively, you can use a food processor.)

2 Stir in the caraway seeds and 45ml/3 tbsp iced water and mix to a firm dough. Knead lightly on a floured surface until smooth.

3 Roll out the pastry and use to line an 18 x 28cm/7 x 11in loose-based flan tin. Reserve the trimmings. Prick the base and chill for 20 minutes. Place a baking sheet in the oven and preheat to 200°C/400°F/Gas 6.

4 Heat the oil in a frying pan and sauté the onions and garlic for 5–6 minutes, until just softened. Remove from the heat and cool.

5 Line the pastry case with grease-proof paper and fill with baking beans. Bake for 10 minutes, then remove the paper and beans and cook for 5 minutes.

6 Mix together the onions, chicken, watercress and lemon rind and spoon into the flan case. Beat the eggs, cream, yogurt, nutmeg, cheese and seasoning and pour over the chicken mix.

7 Roll out the pastry trimmings and cut out 1cm/ ½in strips. Brush with egg, then twist each strip and lay in a lattice over the flan. Press the ends on to the pastry edge. Bake for 35 minutes, until the top is golden. Serve warm or cold.

CAJUN CHICKEN JAMBALAYA

─── INGREDIENTS ───

Serves 4

1.25kg/2½lb fresh chicken
1½ onions
1 bay leaf
4 black peppercorns
1 parsley sprig
30ml/2 tbsp vegetable oil
2 garlic cloves, chopped
1 green pepper, seeded and chopped
1 celery stick, chopped
225g/8oz/1¼ cups long grain rice
115g/4oz/1 cup Chorizo sausage, sliced
115g/4oz/1 cup chopped, cooked ham
400g/14oz can chopped tomatoes with
    herbs
2.5ml/½ tsp hot chilli powder
2.5ml/½ tsp cumin seeds
2.5ml/½ tsp ground cumin
5ml/1 tsp dried thyme
115g/4oz/1 cup cooked, peeled prawns
dash of Tabasco sauce
chopped parsley, to garnish

1 Place the chicken in a large flame-proof casserole and pour over 600ml/1 pint/2½ cups water. Add the half onion, the bay leaf, peppercorns and parsley and bring to the boil. Cover and simmer gently for about 1½ hours.

2 When the chicken is cooked lift it out of the stock, remove the skin and carcass and chop the meat. Strain the stock, leave to cool and reserve.

3 Chop the remaining onion and heat the oil in a large frying pan. Add the onion, garlic, green pepper and celery. Fry for about 5 minutes, then stir in the rice coating the grains with the oil. Add the sausage, ham and reserved chopped chicken and fry for a further 2–3 minutes, stirring frequently.

4 Pour in the tomatoes and 300ml/½ pint/1¼ cups of the reserved stock and add the chilli, cumin, and thyme. Bring to the boil, then cover and simmer gently for 20 minutes, or until the rice is tender and the liquid absorbed.

5 Stir in the prawns and Tabasco. Cook for a further 5 minutes, then season well and serve hot garnished with chopped parsley.

NORMANDY ROAST CHICKEN

Serves 4

50g/2oz/4 tbsp butter, softened
30ml/2 tbsp chopped fresh tarragon
1 small garlic clove, crushed
1.5kg/3lb fresh chicken
5ml/1 tsp plain flour
150ml/¼ pint/⅔ cup single cream or
  crème fraîche
a good squeeze of lemon juice
salt and black pepper
fresh tarragon and lemon slices,
  to garnish

1 Preheat the oven to 200°C/400°F/ Gas 6. Mix together the butter, 15ml/1 tbsp of the chopped tarragon, the garlic and seasoning in a bowl. Spoon half the butter into the cavity of the chicken.

2 Carefully lift the skin at the neck end of the bird away from the breast flesh on each side, then gently push a little of the butter into each pocket and smooth down over the breast with your fingers.

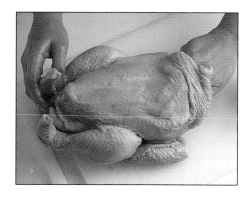

3 Season the bird and lay it, breast down, in a roasting tin. Roast in the oven for 45 minutes, then turn the chicken over and baste with the juices. Cook for a further 45 minutes.

4 When the chicken is cooked, lift it to drain out any juices from the cavity into the tin, then transfer the bird to a warmed platter.

5 Place the roasting tin on the hob and heat until sizzling. Stir in the flour and cook for 1 minute, then stir in the cream, the remaining tarragon, 150ml/¼ pint/⅔ cup water, the lemon juice and seasoning. Boil and stir for 2–3 minutes, until thickened. Garnish the chicken with tarragon and lemon slices and serve with the sauce.

DUCK BREASTS WITH ORANGE SAUCE

A simple variation on the classic French whole roast duck.

Serves 4

4 duck breasts
15ml/1 tbsp sunflower oil
2 oranges
150ml/¼ pint/⅔ cup fresh orange juice
15ml/1 tbsp port
30ml/2 tbsp Seville orange marmalade
15g/½oz/1 tbsp butter
5ml/1 tsp cornflour
salt and black pepper

1 Season the duck breast skin. Heat the oil in a frying pan over a moderate heat and add the duck breasts, skin side down. Cover and cook for 3–4 minutes, until lightly browned. Turn the breasts over, lower the heat slightly and cook uncovered for 5–6 minutes.

2 Peel the skin and pith from the oranges. Working over a bowl to catch any juice, slice either side of the membranes to release the orange segments, then set aside with the juice.

3 Remove the duck breasts from the pan with a slotted spoon, drain on kitchen paper and keep warm in the oven while making the sauce. Drain off the fat from the pan.

4 Add the segmented oranges, all but 30ml/2 tbsp of the orange juice, the port and the orange marmalade to the pan. Bring to the boil and then reduce the heat slightly. Whisk small knobs of the butter into the sauce and season.

5 Blend the cornflour with the reserved orange juice, pour into the pan and stir until slightly thickened. Add the duck breasts and cook gently for about 3 minutes. To serve, arrange the sliced breasts on plates with the sauce.

CRUMBED TURKEY STEAKS

The authentic Austrian recipe for *Weiner Schnitzel* uses veal escalopes (in fact it originally comes from Milan in Italy, where Parmesan cheese replaced the breadcrumbs). Turkey breasts make a tasty alternative.

INGREDIENTS

Serves 4
4 turkey breast steaks (about 150g/5oz each)
45ml/3 tbsp plain flour, seasoned
1 egg, lightly beaten
75g/3oz/1½ cups fresh breadcrumbs
25g/1oz/5 tbsp finely grated Parmesan cheese
25g/1oz/2 tbsp butter
45ml/3 tbsp sunflower oil
fresh parsley, to garnish
4 lemon wedges, to serve

1 Lay the turkey steaks between two sheets of clear film. Bash each one with a rolling pin until flattened. Snip the edges of the steaks with scissors a few times to prevent them curling during cooking.

2 Place the seasoned flour on one plate, the egg into another and the breadcrumbs and Parmesan mixed together on a third plate.

3 Dip each side of the steaks into the flour and shake off any excess. Next, dip them into the egg and then gently press each side into the breadcrumbs and cheese until evenly coated.

4 Heat the butter and oil in a large frying pan and fry the turkey steaks on a moderate heat for 2–3 minutes on each side, until golden. Garnish with parsley and serve with lemon wedges.

COUNTRY CIDER HOT-POT

Game casseroles are popular all over the British Isles.

INGREDIENTS

Serves 4
30ml/2 tbsp plain flour
4 boneless rabbit portions
25g/1oz/2 tbsp butter
15ml/1 tbsp vegetable oil
15 baby onions
4 rashers streaky bacon, chopped
10ml/2 tsp Dijon mustard
450ml/¾ pint/1⅞ cups dry cider
3 carrots, chopped
2 parsnips, chopped
12 ready-to-eat prunes, stoned
1 fresh rosemary sprig
1 bay leaf
salt and black pepper

1 Preheat the oven to 160°C/325°F/ Gas 3. Place the flour and seasoning in a plastic bag, add the rabbit portions and shake until coated. Set aside.

2 Heat the butter and oil in a flame-proof casserole and add the onions and bacon. Fry for 4 minutes, until the onions have softened. Remove with a draining spoon and reserve.

3 Fry the seasoned rabbit portions in the oil in the flameproof casserole until they are browned all over, then spread a little of the mustard over the top of each portion.

4 Return the onions and bacon to the pan. Pour on the cider and add the carrots, parsnips, prunes, rosemary and bay leaf. Season well. Bring to the boil, then cover and transfer to the oven. Cook for about 1½ hours until tender.

5 Remove the rosemary sprig and bay leaf and serve the rabbit hot with creamy mashed potatoes.

FISH AND SEAFOOD

There is nothing quite like the taste of freshly cooked fish and seafood. This chapter is packed with a host of recipes, from the simple to the sophisticated. There's no doubt that after tasting them you will find you could quite happily survive a meat shortage crisis! Try chunky Mediterranean Fish Stew topped with a pungent rouille sauce, Mussels with Wine and Garlic served with crusty French bread, or that great British favourite, Deep-fried Spicy Whitebait. Spanish Seafood Paella, and Sizzling Chinese Steamed Fish are both dinner-party winners, while you can tempt the family with Tuna Fishcake Bites, Baked Fish Creole-Style, or Spaghetti with Seafood Sauce for supper.

MEDITERRANEAN FISH STEW

INGREDIENTS

Serves 4

225g/8oz/2 cups cooked prawns in
  shells
450g/1lb mixed white fish fillets such as
  cod, whiting, haddock, mullet or
  monkfish skinned and chopped
  (reserve skins for the stock)
45ml/3 tbsp olive oil
1 onion, chopped
1 leek, sliced
1 carrot, diced
1 garlic clove, chopped
2.5ml/½ tsp ground turmeric
150ml/¼ pint/⅔ cup dry white wine or
  cider
400g/14oz can chopped tomatoes
sprig of fresh parsley, thyme and fennel
1 bay leaf
a small piece of orange peel
1 prepared squid, body cut into rings
  and tentacles chopped
12 mussels in shells
salt and black pepper
30–45ml/2–3 tbsp Parmesan cheese
  shavings, to sprinkle
chopped fresh parsley, to garnish

For the rouille sauce
2 slices white bread, crusts removed
2 garlic cloves, crushed
½ fresh red chilli
15ml/1 tbsp tomato purée
45–60ml/3–4 tbsp olive oil

1 Peel the prawns leaving the tails on;
cover and chill. Place all the prawn
trimmings and fish trimmings in a pan
and cover with 450ml/¾ pint/1⅞ cups
water. Bring to the boil, then cover and
simmer for about 30 minutes. Strain
and reserve the stock.

2 Heat the oil in a large saucepan and
add the onion, leek, carrot and
garlic. Fry gently for 6–7 minutes, then
stir in the turmeric. Pour on the white
wine, tomatoes and juice, the reserved
fish stock, the herbs and orange peel.
Bring to the boil, then cover and simmer
gently for about 20 minutes.

3 Meanwhile, prepare the rouille
sauce. Blend the bread in a food
processor with the garlic, chilli and
tomato purée. With the motor running,
pour in the oil in a thin drizzle until the
mixture is smooth and thickened.

4 Add the fish and seafood to the pan
and simmer for 5–6 minutes, or
until the fish is opaque and the mussels
open. Remove the bay leaf and peel.
Season the stew and serve in bowls with
a spoonful of the rouille sauce, and
sprinkled with Parmesan and parsley.

SCOTTISH SALMON WITH HERB BUTTER

Serves 4
50g/2oz/4 tbsp butter, softened
finely grated rind of ½ small lemon
15ml/1 tbsp lemon juice
15ml/1 tbsp chopped fresh dill
4 salmon steaks
2 lemon slices, halved
4 fresh dill sprigs
salt and black pepper

1 Place the butter, lemon rind, lemon juice, chopped dill and seasoning in a small bowl and mix together with a fork until blended.

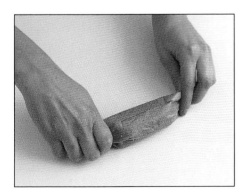

2 Spoon the butter on to a piece of greaseproof paper and roll up, smoothing with your hands into a sausage shape. Twist the ends tightly, wrap in clear film and pop in the freezer for 20 minutes, until firm.

COOK'S TIP
Other fresh herbs could be used to flavour the butter – try mint, fennel fronds, lemon balm, parsley or oregano instead of the dill.

3 Meanwhile, preheat the oven to 190°C/375°F/Gas 5. Cut out four squares of foil big enough to encase the salmon steaks and grease lightly. Place a salmon steak in the centre of each one.

4 Remove the butter from the freezer and slice into eight rounds. Place two rounds on top of each salmon steak with a halved lemon slice in the centre and a sprig of dill on top. Lift up the edges of the foil and crinkle them together until well sealed.

5 Lift the parcels on to a baking sheet and bake for about 20 minutes. Remove from the oven and place the unopened parcels on warmed plates. Open the parcels and slide the contents on to the plates with the juices.

Chinese Omelettes with Fried Rice

Makes 4

30ml/2 tbsp sesame oil
30ml/2 tbsp sesame seeds
225g/8oz/1¼ cups cooked long grain
    rice
5cm/2in piece of cucumber, finely
    grated
5ml/1 tsp finely grated lemon rind
squeeze of lemon juice
6 eggs
15ml/1 tbsp dry sherry
15ml/1 tbsp light soy sauce
pinch of caster sugar
225g/8oz/2 cups cooked peeled prawns
4 spring onions, finely chopped
2 large tomatoes, seeded and chopped
30ml/2 tbsp vegetable oil
salt and black pepper
4 cooked prawns in shells and fresh
    coriander sprigs, to garnish

1 Heat the sesame oil in a pan and fry the sesame seeds until golden. Stir in the cooked rice, followed by the cucumber, lemon rind and juice and seasoning. Cook for 2–3 minutes, then keep warm while making the omelettes.

2 Place the eggs, sherry, soy sauce, sugar and a little pepper into a bowl and beat with a fork. Stir in the peeled prawns, spring onions and tomatoes.

3 Heat 7.5ml/½ tbsp of the oil in frying pan and ladle in a quarter of the mixture. Fry over a moderate heat for 3–4 minutes, until the omelette is lightly golden underneath. Cover and cook until the omelette is just set.

4 Remove the lid and fold the omelette in half. Garnish with a prawn and fresh coriander and serve with a spoonful of the rice. Make the remaining omelettes in the same way.

Sizzling Chinese Steamed Fish

Steamed whole fish is very popular in China and the wok is used as a steamer. In this recipe the fish is flavoured with garlic, ginger and spring onions cooked in sizzling hot oil.

Serves 4

4 rainbow trout (about 250g/9oz each)
1.25ml/¼ tsp salt
2.5ml/½ tsp sugar
2 garlic cloves, finely chopped
15ml/1 tbsp finely diced fresh root
    ginger
5 spring onions, cut into 5cm/2in
    lengths and finely shredded
60ml/4 tbsp groundnut oil
5ml/1 tsp sesame oil
45ml/3 tbsp light soy sauce
thread egg noodles, to serve

1 Make three diagonal slits on both sides of each fish and lay them on a heatproof plate. Place a small rack or trivet in a wok or large frying pan half filled with water, cover and heat until just simmering.

2 Sprinkle the fish with the salt, sugar, garlic and ginger. Sit the plate on the rack and cover. Steam gently for about 10–12 minutes, or until the flesh has turned pale pink and feels quite firm.

3 Turn off the heat, remove the lid and scatter the spring onions over the fish. Replace the lid.

4 Heat the oils in a small pan over a high heat until just smoking, then quickly pour a quarter over the spring onions on each of the fish – the shredded onions will sizzle and cook in the hot oil – then sprinkle the soy sauce over the top. Serve the fish and juices immediately with boiled noodles.

Spanish Seafood Paella

Serves 4

60ml/4 tbsp olive oil

225g/8oz monkfish or cod, skinned and cut into chunks

3 prepared baby squid, body cut into rings and tentacles chopped

1 red mullet, filleted, skinned and cut into chunks (optional)

1 onion, chopped

3 garlic cloves, finely chopped

1 red pepper, seeded and sliced

4 tomatoes, skinned and chopped

225g/8oz/1¼ cups arborio rice

450ml/¾ pint/1⅞ cups fish stock

150ml/¼ pint/⅔ cup white wine

75g/3oz/¾ cup frozen peas

4–5 saffron strands soaked in 30ml/ 2 tbsp hot water

115g/4oz/1 cup cooked peeled prawns

8 fresh mussels in shells, scrubbed

salt and pepper

15ml/1 tbsp chopped fresh parsley, to garnish

lemon wedges, to serve

1 Heat 30ml/2 tbsp of the oil in a large frying pan and add the monkfish or cod, the squid and the red mullet, if using, to the pan. Stir-fry for 2 minutes, then transfer the fish to a bowl with all the juices and reserve.

2 Heat the remaining 30ml/2 tbsp of oil in the pan and add the onion, garlic and pepper. Fry for 6–7 minutes, stirring frequently, until the onions and peppers have softened.

3 Stir in the tomatoes and fry for 2 minutes, then add the rice, stirring to coat the grains with oil, and cook for 2–3 minutes. Pour on the fish stock and wine and add the peas, saffron and water. Season well and mix.

4 Gently stir in the reserved cooked fish with all the juices, followed by the prawns and then push the mussels into the rice. Cover and cook over a gentle heat for about 30 minutes, or until the stock has been absorbed but the mixture is still moist.

5 Remove from the heat, keep covered and leave to stand for 5 minutes. Sprinkle with parsley and serve with lemon wedges.

SPAGHETTI WITH SEAFOOD SAUCE

The Italian name for this tomato-based sauce is *marinara*.

INGREDIENTS

Serves 4
45ml/3 tbsp olive oil
1 medium onion, chopped
1 garlic clove, finely chopped
225g/8oz spaghetti
600ml/1 pint/2½ cups passata
15ml/1 tbsp tomato purée
5ml/1 tsp dried oregano
1 bay leaf
5ml/1 tsp sugar
115g/4oz/1 cup cooked peeled shrimps
   (rinsed well if canned)
115g/4oz/1 cup cooked peeled prawns
175g/6oz/1½ cups cooked clam or
   cockle meat (rinsed well if canned or
   bottled)
15ml/1 tbsp lemon juice
45ml/3 tbsp chopped fresh parsley
25g/1oz/2 tbsp butter
salt and black pepper
4 whole cooked prawns, to garnish

1 Heat the oil in a pan and add the onion and garlic. Fry over a moderate heat for 6–7 minutes, until the onions have softened.

2 Meanwhile, cook the spaghetti in a large pan of boiling salted water for 10–12 minutes until *al dente*.

3 Stir the passata, tomato purée, oregano, bay leaf and sugar into the onions and season well. Bring to the boil, then simmer for 2–3 minutes.

4 Add the shellfish, lemon juice and 30ml/2 tbsp of the parsley. Stir well, then cover and cook for 6–7 minutes.

5 Meanwhile, drain the spaghetti when it is ready and add the butter to the pan. Return the drained spaghetti to the pan and toss in the butter. Season well.

6 Divide the spaghetti among four warmed plates and top with the seafood sauce. Sprinkle with the remaining 15ml/1 tbsp parsley, garnish with whole prawns and serve immediately.

DEEP-FRIED SPICY WHITEBAIT

A delicious British dish – serve these tiny fish very hot and crisp.

INGREDIENTS

Serves 4
450g/1lb whitebait
45ml/3 tbsp plain flour
5ml/1 tsp paprika
pinch of cayenne pepper
12 fresh sprigs parsley
vegetable oil, for deep-frying
salt and black pepper
4 lemon wedges, to garnish

1 If using frozen whitebait, defrost in the bag, drain off any water. Spread the fish on kitchen paper and pat dry.

2 Place the flour, paprika, cayenne and seasoning in a large plastic bag. Add the whitebait and shake gently until all the fish are lightly coated with the flour. Transfer to a plate.

3 Heat about 5cm/2in of oil in a pan or deep-fat fryer to 190°C/375°F, or until a cube of bread dropped in browns in 30 seconds.

4 Add the whitebait in batches and deep-fry in the hot oil for 2–3 minutes, until the coating is lightly golden and crispy. Remove, drain on kitchen paper and keep warm in the oven while frying the remainder.

5 When all the whitebait is cooked, drop the sprigs of parsley into the hot oil (don't worry if the oil spits a bit) and fry for a few seconds until crisp. Drain on kitchen paper. Serve the whitebait garnished with the deep-fried parsley sprigs and lemon wedges.

PORTUGUESE GRILLED SARDINES

INGREDIENTS

Serves 4
8–12 fresh sardines (depending on size)
75ml/5 tbsp olive oil
juice of 1 lemon
5ml/1 tsp finely grated lemon rind
30ml/2 tbsp chopped fresh parsley
salt and black pepper
4 lemon wedges, tomato salad and hot garlic bread, to serve

1 First of all, remove the scales by holding the fish by their tails under running water and gently rubbing the skin with your fingers from the tail towards the head. Make a slit in the belly and remove the innards, rinse the fish and pat dry with kitchen paper. Make two diagonal slashes in the skin on both sides of each sardine and transfer to a plate.

2 Preheat the grill. Mix together the oil, lemon juice, lemon rind, parsley and seasoning. Brush the fish with the marinade and place on a grill rack.

3 Cook under a moderate heat for about 2–3 minutes, basting once, until the skin is starting to crispen and then carefully turn the fish over. Brush with some more of the marinade. Grill for a further 2–3 minutes.

4 Lift the sardines carefully on to a warmed serving platter and pour over the remaining marinade. Serve with lemon wedges, a tomato salad and hot crusty garlic bread.

> **COOK'S TIP**
> Sardines are baby pilchards and can be rather bony – so beware. Always choose firm, fresh fish. Bright eyes are a sign of freshness.

BAKED FISH CREOLE-STYLE

INGREDIENTS

Serves 4

15ml/1 tbsp oil
25g/1oz/2 tbsp butter
1 onion, thinly sliced
1 garlic clove, chopped
1 red pepper, seeded, halved and sliced
1 green pepper, seeded, halved and sliced
400g/14oz can chopped tomatoes with basil
15ml/1 tbsp tomato purée
30ml/2 tbsp capers, chopped
3–4 drops Tabasco sauce
4 tail end pieces cod or haddock fillets (about 175g/6oz each), skinned
6 basil leaves, shredded
45ml/3 tbsp fresh breadcrumbs
25g/1oz/¼ cup grated Cheddar cheese
10ml/2 tsp chopped fresh parsley
salt and black pepper
fresh basil sprigs, to garnish

1 Preheat the oven to 230°C/450°F/ Gas 8. Butter an ovenproof dish.

2 Heat the oil and half the butter in a pan and add the onion. Fry for about 6–7 minutes, until softened, then add the garlic, peppers, chopped tomatoes, tomato purée, capers and Tabasco and season well. Cover and cook for 15 minutes, then uncover and simmer gently for 5 minutes to reduce slightly.

3 Place the fish fillets in the ovenproof dish, dot with the remaining 15g/½oz/1 tbsp butter and season lightly. Spoon over the tomato and pepper sauce and sprinkle over the shredded basil. Bake in the oven for about 10 minutes.

4 Meanwhile, mix together the breadcrumbs, cheese and parsley in a bowl.

5 Remove the fish from the oven and scatter the cheese and breadcrumbs over the top. Return to the oven and bake for a further 10 minutes, until lightly browned.

6 Let the fish stand for about a minute, then, using a fish slice, carefully transfer each topped fillet to warmed plates. Garnish with sprigs of fresh basil and serve hot.

TUNA FISHCAKE BITES

An updated version of a traditional British tea-time dish.

INGREDIENTS

Serves 4
675g/1½lb (about 5 medium) potatoes
knob of butter
2 hard-boiled eggs, chopped
3 spring onions, finely chopped
finely grated rind of ½ lemon
5ml/1 tsp lemon juice
30ml/2 tbsp chopped fresh parsley
200g/7oz can tuna in oil, drained
10ml/2 tsp capers, chopped
2 eggs, lightly beaten
115g/4oz/2 cups fresh white bread-
    crumbs, for coating
sunflower oil, for frying
salt and black pepper
mixed salad, to serve

For the tartare sauce
60ml/4 tbsp mayonnaise
15ml/1 tbsp natural yogurt
15ml/1 tbsp finely chopped gherkins
15ml/1 tbsp capers, chopped
15ml/1 tbsp chopped fresh parsley

1 Cook the potatoes in a pan of boiling salted water until tender. Drain well, add the butter and mash well. Leave to cool.

2 Add the hard-boiled eggs, spring onions, lemon rind, lemon juice, parsley, tuna, capers and 15ml/1 tbsp of the beaten egg to the cooled potato. Mix well with a fork and season. Cover and chill for about 30 minutes.

3 Meanwhile, place all the ingredients for the tartare sauce in a bowl and mix well. Chill and reserve.

4 Pour the remaining beaten egg into one shallow bowl and the breadcrumbs into another. Roll the chilled fishcake mixture into about 24 balls. Dip these into the egg and then roll gently in the breadcrumbs until evenly coated. Transfer to a plate.

5 Heat 90ml/6 tbsp of oil in a frying pan and fry the balls on a moderate heat, in batches, for about 4 minutes, turning two or three times until browned all over. Drain on kitchen paper and keep warm in the oven while frying the remainder.

6 Serve about six balls per person with the tartare sauce and a salad.

KASHMIR COCONUT FISH CURRY

INGREDIENTS

Serves 4

30ml/2 tbsp vegetable oil
2 onions, sliced
1 green pepper, seeded and sliced
1 garlic clove, crushed
1 dried chilli, seeded and chopped
5ml/1 tsp ground coriander
5ml/1 tsp ground cumin
2.5ml/½ tsp ground turmeric
2.5ml/½ tsp hot chilli powder
2.5ml/½ tsp garam masala
15ml/1 tbsp plain flour
115g/4oz creamed coconut, chopped
*675g/1½lb haddock fillet, skinned and
   chopped*
*4 tomatoes, skinned, seeded and
   chopped*
15ml/1 tbsp lemon juice
30ml/2 tbsp ground almonds
30ml/2 tbsp double cream
fresh coriander sprigs, to garnish
naan bread and boiled rice, to serve

1 Heat the oil in a large saucepan and add the onions, pepper and garlic. Cook for 6–7 minutes, until the onions and peppers have softened. Stir in the chopped dried chilli, all the ground spices, the chilli powder, garam masala and flour, and cook for 1 minute.

2 Dissolve the coconut in 600ml/ 1 pint/2½ cups boiling water and stir into the spicy vegetable mixture. Bring to the boil, cover and then simmer gently for 6 minutes.

3 Add the fish and tomatoes and cook for about 5–6 minutes, or until the fish has turned opaque. Uncover and gently stir in the lemon juice, ground almonds and cream. Season well, garnish with coriander and serve with naan bread and rice.

> **COOK'S TIP**
> Replace the haddock with any firm fleshed white fish such as cod or whiting. Stir in a few cooked, peeled prawns, if you like.

MUSSELS WITH WINE AND GARLIC

This famous French dish is traditionally known as *moules marinière*.

INGREDIENTS

Serves 4

*1.75kg/4lb (about 4 pints) fresh
   mussels in shells*
15ml/1 tbsp oil
25g/1oz/2 tbsp butter
*1 small onion or 2 shallots, finely
   chopped*
2 garlic cloves, finely chopped
*150ml/¼ pint/⅔ cup dry white wine
   or cider*
fresh parsley sprigs
black pepper
*30ml/2 tbsp chopped fresh parsley,
   to garnish*
French bread, to serve

1 Check that the mussels are closed. (Throw away any that are cracked or won't close when tapped.) Scrape the shells under cold running water and pull off the hairy beard attached to the hinge of the shell. Rinse well in two or three changes of water.

2 Heat the oil and butter in a large pan, add the onions and garlic and fry for 3–4 minutes.

3 Pour on the wine or cider and add the parsley sprigs, stir well, bring to the boil, then add the mussels. Cover and cook for about 5–7 minutes, shaking the pan once or twice until the shells open (throw away any that have not).

4 Serve the mussels and their juices sprinkled with the chopped parsley and a few grinds of black pepper. Accompany with hot French bread.

THAI PRAWN SALAD

This salad has the distinctive flavour of lemon grass, the bulbous grass used widely in South-east Asian cooking.

INGREDIENTS

Serves 4 as a starter

250g/9oz cooked, peeled extra large
    tiger prawns
15ml/1 tbsp oriental fish sauce
30ml/2 tbsp lime juice
7.5ml/½ tsp soft light brown sugar
1 small fresh red chilli, finely chopped
1 spring onion, finely chopped
1 small garlic clove, crushed
2.5cm/1in piece fresh lemon grass,
    finely chopped
30ml/2 tbsp chopped fresh coriander
45ml/3 tbsp dry white wine
8–12 Little Gem lettuce leaves, to serve
fresh coriander sprigs, to garnish

1 Place the tiger prawns in a bowl and add all the remaining ingredients. Stir well, cover and leave to marinate in the fridge for 2–3 hours, mixing and turning the prawns occasionally.

2 Arrange two or three of the lettuce leaves on each of four individual serving plates.

3 Spoon the prawn salad into the lettuce leaves. Garnish with fresh coriander and serve at once.

COOK'S TIP
If you find raw prawns, cook them in boiling water until pink and use instead of the cooked prawns.

CAJUN SPICED FISH

Cajun blackened fish is a speciality of Paul Prudhommes, a chef from New Orleans. Fillets of fish are coated with an aromatic blend of herbs and spices and pan-fried in butter.

INGREDIENTS

Serves 4

5ml/1 tsp dried thyme
5ml/1 tsp dried oregano
5ml/1 tsp ground black pepper
1.25ml/¼ tsp cayenne pepper
10ml/2 tsp paprika
2.5ml/½ tsp garlic salt
4 tail end pieces of cod fillet
    (about 175g/6oz each)
75g/3oz/6 tbsp butter
½ red pepper, sliced
½ green pepper, sliced
fresh thyme, to garnish
grilled tomatoes and sweet potato
    purée, to serve

1 Place all the herbs and spices in a bowl and mix well. Dip the fish fillets in the spice mixture until lightly coated.

2 Heat 25g/1oz/2 tbsp of the butter in a large frying pan, add the peppers and fry for 4–5 minutes, until softened. Remove the peppers and keep warm.

3 Add the remaining butter to the pan and heat until sizzling. Add the cod fillets and fry on a moderate heat for 3–4 minutes on each side, until browned and cooked.

4 Transfer the fish to a warmed serving dish, surround with the peppers and garnish with thyme. Serve the spiced fish with some grilled tomatoes and sweet potato purée.

COOK'S TIP
This blend of herbs and spices can be used to flavour any fish steaks or fillets and could also be used to jazz up pan-fried prawns.

PASTA, PIZZAS AND GRAINS

This chapter is full of recipes that will bring back memories of sunshine holidays all over the world. From Italy comes a favourite recipe for Spinach and Cheese Dumplings drenched in a lemon and basil butter, as well as a classic creamy Asparagus and Cheese Risotto, and a Roman recipe for Pasta Carbonara. For pizza lovers there is a thick-crusted variety packed with spicy peperoni and sweet peppers, and a French Onion Tart from the heart of Provence. For a cold meal, the Middle Eastern Lemony Bulgar Wheat Salad is easy and delicious. From Morocco, steamed couscous topped with honeyed chicken makes the ideal dinner-party dish. For speedy stir-fried meals, go for the Far Eastern Thai Fried Noodles, and Chinese Special Fried Rice – versatile recipes where the ingredients are infinitely variable.

PEPERONI PIZZA

INGREDIENTS

Makes a 30cm/12in pizza
For the sauce
30ml/2 tbsp olive oil
1 onion, finely chopped
1 garlic clove, crushed
400g/14oz can chopped tomatoes
  with herbs
15ml/1 tbsp tomato purée

For the pizza base
275g/10oz/2½ cups plain flour
2.5ml/½ tsp salt
5ml/1 tsp easy-blend yeast
30ml/2 tbsp olive oil

For the topping
½ red pepper, sliced into rings
½ yellow pepper, sliced into rings
½ green pepper, sliced into rings
150g/5oz mozzarella cheese, sliced
75g/3oz/½ cup peperoni sausage,
  thinly sliced
8 black olives, stoned
3 sun-dried tomatoes, chopped
2.5ml/½ tsp dried oregano
olive oil, for drizzling

1 To make the sauce, heat the oil in a saucepan and add the onions and garlic. Fry gently for about 6–7 minutes, until softened. Add the tomatoes and stir in the tomato purée. Bring to the boil and boil rapidly for 5 minutes, until reduced slightly. Remove the pan from the heat and leave to cool.

2 For the pizza base, lightly grease a 30cm/12in round pizza tray. Sift the flour and salt into a bowl. Sprinkle over the easy-blend yeast and make a well in the centre. Pour in 175ml/6fl oz/¾ cup warm water and the olive oil. Mix to a soft dough.

3 Place the dough on a lightly floured surface and knead for about 5–10 minutes, until smooth. Roll out to a 25cm/10in round, making the edges slightly thicker than the centre. Lift the dough on to the pizza tray.

4 Spread the tomato sauce over the dough and then top with the peppers, mozzarella, peperoni, black olives and tomatoes. Sprinkle over the oregano and drizzle with olive oil. Cover loosely and leave in a warm place for 30 minutes, until slightly risen. Meanwhile, preheat the oven to 220°C/425°F/Gas 7.

5 Bake for 25–30 minutes and serve hot straight from the tray.

BROCCOLI AND RICOTTA CANNELLONI

INGREDIENTS

Serves 4

12 dried cannelloni tubes, 7.5cm/
   3in long
450g/1lb/4 cups broccoli florets
75g/3oz/1½ cups fresh breadcrumbs
150ml/¼ pint/⅔ cup milk
60ml/4 tbsp olive oil, plus extra for
   brushing
225g/8oz/1 cup ricotta cheese
pinch of grated nutmeg
90ml/6 tbsp grated Parmesan or
   Pecorino cheese
salt and black pepper
30ml/2 tbsp pine nuts, for sprinkling

For the tomato sauce

30ml/2 tbsp olive oil
1 onion, finely chopped
1 garlic clove, crushed
2 x 400g/14oz cans chopped tomatoes
15ml/1 tbsp tomato purée
4 black olives, stoned and chopped
5ml/1 tsp dried thyme

1 Preheat the oven to 190°C/375°F/
Gas 5 and lightly grease an oven-proof dish with olive oil. Bring a large saucepan of water to the boil, add a little olive oil and simmer the cannelloni, uncovered, for about 6–7 minutes, or until nearly cooked.

2 Meanwhile, steam or boil the broccoli for 10 minutes, until tender. Drain the pasta, rinse under cold water and reserve. Drain the broccoli and leave to cool, then place in a food processor or blender, whizz until smooth and set aside.

3 Place the breadcrumbs in a bowl, add the milk and oil and stir until softened. Add the ricotta, broccoli purée, nutmeg, 60ml/4 tbsp of the Parmesan cheese and seasoning, then set aside.

4 To make the sauce, heat the oil in a frying pan and add the onions and garlic. Fry for 5–6 minutes, until softened, then stir in the tomatoes, tomato purée, black olives, thyme and seasoning. Boil rapidly for 2–3 minutes, then pour into the base of the dish.

5 Spoon the cheese mixture into a piping bag fitted with a 1cm/½in nozzle. Carefully open the cannelloni tubes. Standing each one upright on a board, pipe the filling into each tube. Lay them in rows in the tomato sauce.

6 Brush the tops of the cannelloni with a little olive oil and sprinkle over the remaining Parmesan cheese and pine nuts. Bake in the oven for about 25–30 minutes, until golden on top.

ITALIAN PASTA WITH PESTO SAUCE

Serves 4

a little olive oil
350g/12oz fresh paglia e fieno pasta
4 sun-dried tomatoes in oil, chopped
Parmesan cheese shavings (made using a potato peeler) and fresh basil sprigs, to garnish
French bread, to serve

For the pesto

25g/1oz/¼ cup pine nuts
25g/1oz/2 cups fresh parsley sprigs
25g/1oz/2 cups fresh basil leaves
2 garlic cloves, chopped
175ml/6fl oz/¾ cup olive oil
90ml/6 tbsp finely grated Pecorino or Parmesan cheese
salt and black pepper

1 Place the pine nuts in a small frying pan and dry-fry until lightly browned all over. When cooled, place in a food processor or blender with the parsley, basil and garlic and pulse until finely chopped.

2 With the motor running, slowly pour on the olive oil in a thin stream and the mixture will thicken.

3 Finally add the grated cheese and pulse for a few short bursts until well mixed in. Season and set aside.

4 Bring a large pan of salted water to the boil and add a little olive oil. Add the fresh pasta and cook for 5–6 minutes, until *al dente*. Drain well and return to the pan.

5 Stir in the pesto sauce and mix well until all the pasta is thoroughly coated. Divide between warmed individual serving bowls and top with chopped sun-dried tomatoes, Parmesan cheese shavings and a sprig of fresh basil. Serve with hot French bread.

FRENCH ONION TART

Serves 6

30ml/2 tbsp olive oil
6 medium onions, thinly sliced
2 garlic cloves, crushed

For the dough

275g/10oz packet pizza base mix
5ml/1 tsp olive oil
50g/2oz can anchovy fillets (about 12), sliced in half lengthways
8 black olives, stoned
10ml/2 tsp chopped fresh thyme, or 2.5ml/½ tsp dried thyme
salt and black pepper

1 Heat the oil in a frying pan, add the sliced onions and garlic and season lightly. Fry gently, stirring occasionally, for about 40 minutes, or until the onions are soft but not too brown.

2 Preheat the oven to 220°C/425°F/ Gas 7. Empty the pizza base mix into a bowl, stir in 250ml/8fl oz/1 cup warm water and add the oil. Mix to a dough and knead for about 5 minutes.

3 Lightly grease a 33 x 23cm/13 x 9in Swiss roll tin. Roll the dough out on a lightly floured surface to fit the tin and press into the base. Spread the cooked onions evenly over the dough base and then arrange the anchovies on top in a lattice pattern.

4 Scatter over the olives and chopped thyme and drizzle with a little more olive oil. Place in a large sealed plastic bag and leave to rise in a warm place for 15 minutes.

5 Bake for 10 minutes, then reduce the temperature to 190°C/375°F/ Gas 5 and cook for 15–20 minutes, or until golden brown around the edges. Cut into six pieces and serve warm or cold.

ASPARAGUS AND CHEESE RISOTTO

An authentic Italian risotto has a unique creamy texture achieved by constant stirring of the arborio rice, available from good supermarkets or delicatessens.

INGREDIENTS

Serves 4

1.25ml/¼ tsp saffron strands
750ml/1¼ pints/3⅔ cups hot chicken stock
25g/1oz/2 tbsp butter
30ml/2 tbsp olive oil
1 large onion, finely chopped
2 garlic cloves, finely chopped
225g/8oz/1¼ cups arborio rice
300ml/½ pint/1¼ cups dry white wine
225g/8 oz asparagus tips (or asparagus cut into 5cm/2in lengths), cooked
75g/3oz/1 cup finely grated Parmesan cheese
salt and black pepper
Parmesan shavings and fresh basil sprigs, to garnish
ciabatta bread rolls and salad, to serve

1 Sprinkle the saffron over the stock and leave to stand for 5 minutes.

2 Heat the butter and oil in a frying pan, add the onions and garlic. Fry for about 6 minutes, until softened.

3 Add the rice and stir-fry for 1–2 minutes to coat the grains with the butter and oil.

4 Pour on 300ml/½ pint/1¼ cups of the hot chicken stock and saffron. Cook gently over a moderate heat, stirring frequently, until all the liquid has been absorbed.

5 Repeat with another 300ml/½ pint/1¼ cups stock. When that has been absorbed, add the wine and carry on cooking and stirring until the rice has a creamy consistency.

6 Add the asparagus and remaining stock and stir until the liquid is absorbed and the rice is tender. Stir in the Parmesan cheese and season well.

7 Spoon the risotto on to warmed plates and garnish with the Parmesan cheese shavings and fresh basil. Serve with hot ciabatta rolls and a crisp green salad.

MOROCCAN CHICKEN COUSCOUS

Serves 4

15ml/1 tbsp butter
15ml/1 tbsp sunflower oil
4 chicken portions
2 onions, finely chopped
2 garlic cloves, crushed
2.5ml/½ tsp ground cinnamon
1.25ml/¼ tsp ground ginger
1.25ml/¼ tsp ground turmeric
30ml/2 tbsp orange juice
10ml/2 tsp clear honey
salt and black pepper
fresh mint sprigs, to garnish

For the couscous

350g/12oz/2¼ cups couscous
5ml/1 tsp salt
10ml/2 tsp caster sugar
30ml/2 tbsp sunflower oil
2.5ml/½ tsp ground cinnamon
pinch of grated nutmeg
15ml/1 tbsp orange blossom water
30ml/2 tbsp sultanas
50g/2oz/½ cup chopped blanched
   almonds
45ml/3 tbsp chopped pistachio nuts

1 Heat the butter and oil in a large pan and add the chicken portions, skin side down. Fry for 3–4 minutes, until the skin is golden, then turn over.

2 Add the onions, garlic, spices and a pinch of salt and pour over the orange juice and 300ml/½ pint/1¼ cups of water. Cover and bring to the boil, then reduce the heat and simmer for about 30 minutes.

3 Meanwhile, place the couscous and salt in a bowl and cover with 350ml/12fl oz/1½ cups water. Stir once and leave to stand for 5 minutes. Add the caster sugar, 15ml/1 tbsp of the oil, the cinnamon, nutmeg, orange blossom water and sultanas to the couscous and mix very well.

4 Heat the remaining 15ml/1 tbsp of the oil in a pan and lightly fry the almonds until golden. Stir into the couscous with the pistachio nuts.

5 Line a steamer with greaseproof paper and spoon in the couscous. Sit the steamer over the chicken (or over a pan of boiling water) and steam for 10 minutes.

6 Remove the steamer and keep covered. Stir the honey into the chicken liquid and boil rapidly for 3–4 minutes. Spoon the couscous on to a warmed serving platter and top with the chicken, with a little of the sauce spooned over. Garnish with fresh mint and serve with the remaining sauce.

PASTA CARBONARA

An Italian favourite and a classic Roman dish, whose name translates as 'charcoal burners' pasta'. Traditionally made with spaghetti, it is equally delicious with fresh egg tagliatelle.

INGREDIENTS

Serves 4

350–450g/12oz–1lb fresh tagliatelle
15ml/1 tbsp olive oil
225g/8oz piece of ham, bacon or pancetta, cut into 2.5cm/1in sticks
115g/4oz (about 10) button mushrooms, sliced
4 eggs, lightly beaten
75ml/5 tbsp single cream
salt and black pepper
30ml/2 tbsp finely grated Parmesan cheese
fresh basil sprigs, to garnish

1 Cook the pasta in a pan of boiling salted water, with a little oil added, for 6–8 minutes or until *al dente*.

2 Meanwhile, heat the oil in a frying pan and add the ham. Fry for 3–4 minutes and then add the mushrooms and fry for a further 3–4 minutes. Turn off the heat and reserve. Lightly beat the eggs and cream together in a bowl and season well.

3 When the pasta is cooked, drain it well and return to the pan. Add the ham, mushrooms and any pan juices and stir into the pasta.

4 Pour in the eggs and cream and half the Parmesan cheese. Stir well and as you do this the eggs will cook in the heat of the pasta. Pile on to warmed serving plates, sprinkle with the remaining Parmesan and garnish with basil.

BAKED MACARONI CHEESE

A British supper-time dish – replace the Cheddar with your family's favourite cheese.

INGREDIENTS

Serves 4

15ml/1 tbsp olive oil
275g/10oz/2⅓ cups macaroni
2 leeks, chopped
50g/2oz/4 tbsp butter
50g/2oz/½ cup plain flour
900ml/1½ pints/3¾ cups milk
225g/8oz/2 cups grated mature Cheddar cheese
30ml/2 tbsp fromage frais
5ml/1 tsp wholegrain mustard
50g/2oz/1 cup fresh breadcrumbs
25g/1oz/½ cup grated Double Gloucester cheese
salt and black pepper
15ml/1 tbsp chopped fresh parsley, to garnish

1 Preheat the oven to 180°C/350°F/Gas 4. Bring a large pan of salted water to the boil and add the olive oil. Add the macaroni and leeks and boil gently for 10 minutes. Drain, rinse under cold water and reserve.

2 Heat the butter in a saucepan, stir in the flour and cook for about a minute. Remove from the heat and gradually add the milk, stirring well after each addition until smooth. Return to the heat and stir continuously until thickened.

3 Add the Cheddar cheese, fromage frais and mustard, mix well, and season with salt and pepper.

4 Stir the drained macaroni and leeks into the cheese sauce and pile into a greased ovenproof dish. Level the top with the back of a spoon and sprinkle over the breadcrumbs and Double Gloucester cheese.

5 Bake for 35–40 minutes. Serve hot, garnished with fresh parsley.

LOUISIANA RICE

Serves 4

60ml/4 tbsp vegetable oil
1 small aubergine, diced
225g/8oz minced pork
1 green pepper, seeded and chopped
2 sticks celery, chopped
1 onion, chopped
1 garlic clove, crushed
5ml/1 tsp cayenne pepper
5ml/1 tsp paprika
5ml/1 tsp black pepper
2.5ml/½ tsp salt
5ml/1 tsp dried thyme
2.5ml/½ tsp dried oregano
475ml/16fl oz/2 cups chicken stock
225g/8oz chicken livers, minced
150g/5oz/¾ cup long grain rice
1 bay leaf
45ml/3 tbsp chopped fresh parsley
celery leaves, to garnish

1 Heat the oil in a frying pan until really hot, then add the aubergine and stir-fry for about 5 minutes.

2 Add the pork and cook for about 6–8 minutes, until browned, using a wooden spoon to break any lumps.

3 Add the pepper, celery, onion, garlic and all the spices and herbs. Cover and cook on a high heat for 5–6 minutes, stirring frequently from the bottom to scrape up and distribute the crispy brown bits.

4 Pour on the chicken stock and stir to clean the bottom of the pan. Cover and cook for 6 minutes over a moderate heat. Stir in the chicken livers, cook for 2 minutes, then stir in the rice and add the bay leaf.

5 Reduce the heat, cover and simmer for about 6–7 minutes. Turn off the heat and leave to stand for a further 10–15 minutes until the rice is tender. Remove the bay leaf and stir in the chopped parsley. Serve the rice hot, garnished with the celery leaves.

SPINACH AND CHEESE DUMPLINGS

These little dumplings are known as *gnocchi* in Italy.

INGREDIENTS

Serves 4
175g/6oz/1¼ cups cold mashed potato
75g/3oz/½ cup semolina
115g/4oz/1 cup frozen leaf spinach,
   defrosted, squeezed and chopped
115g/4oz/½ cup ricotta cheese
25g/1oz/5 tbsp grated Parmesan cheese
30ml/2 tbsp beaten egg
2.5ml/½ tsp salt
large pinch of grated nutmeg
black pepper
30ml/2 tbsp grated Parmesan cheese
fresh basil sprigs, to garnish

For the butter
75g/3oz/6 tbsp butter
5ml/1 tsp grated lemon rind
15ml/1 tbsp lemon juice
15ml/1 tbsp chopped fresh basil

1 Place all the gnocchi ingredients except the basil in a bowl and mix well. Take small pieces of the mixture, about the size of a walnut, and roll each one back and forth a few times along the prongs of a fork until ridged. Repeat until you have 28 gnocchi and lay on a tray lined with clear film.

2 Bring a large pan of water to the boil, reduce the heat slightly, and drop the gnocchi into the simmering water. They will sink to the bottom at first, but as they cook they will rise to the surface – this will take about 2 minutes, then simmer for about 1 minute.

3 Remove the gnocchi with a slotted spoon and transfer to a lightly greased and warmed ovenproof dish.

4 Sprinkle the gnocchi with a little Parmesan cheese and grill under a high heat for about 2 minutes, or until lightly browned. Meanwhile, heat the butter in a pan and stir in the lemon rind and juice, basil and seasoning.

5 Pour a quarter of the hot butter over each portion of gnocchi and garnish with fresh basil. Serve hot.

CHINESE SPECIAL FRIED RICE

Cooked white rice fried with a selection of other ingredients is a staple Chinese dish. This recipe combines a mixture of chicken, shrimps and vegetables with fried rice.

—INGREDIENTS—

Serves 4

175g/6oz/1 cup long grain white rice
45ml/3 tbsp groundnut oil
1 garlic clove, crushed
4 spring onions, finely chopped
115g/4oz/1 cup diced cooked chicken
115g/4oz/1 cup cooked peeled shrimps
    (rinsed if canned)
50g/2oz/½ cup frozen peas
1 egg, beaten with a pinch of salt
50g/2oz/1 cup lettuce, shredded
30ml/2 tbsp light soy sauce
pinch of caster sugar
salt and black pepper
15ml/1 tbsp chopped, roasted cashew
    nuts, to garnish

1 Rinse the rice in two to three changes of warm water to wash away some of the starch. Drain well.

2 Put the rice in a saucepan and add 15ml/1 tbsp of the oil and 350ml/ 12fl oz/1½ cups of water. Cover and bring to the boil, stir once, then cover and simmer for 12–15 minutes, until nearly all the water has been absorbed. Turn off the heat and leave, covered, to stand for 10 minutes. Fluff up with a fork and leave to cool.

3 Heat the remaining oil in a wok or frying pan, add the garlic and spring onions and stir-fry for 30 seconds.

4 Add the chicken, shrimps and peas and stir-fry for 1–2 minutes, then add the cooked rice and stir-fry for a further 2 minutes. Pour in the egg and stir-fry until just set. Stir in the lettuce, soy sauce, sugar and seasoning.

5 Transfer to a warmed serving bowl, sprinkle with the chopped cashew nuts and serve immediately.

LEMONY BULGUR WHEAT SALAD

This nutty Middle Eastern salad called *Tabbouleh* is delicious as an accompaniment to grilled meats or fish or on its own.

—INGREDIENTS—

Serves 4

225g/8oz/1½ cups bulgur wheat
4 spring onions, finely chopped
75ml/5 tbsp chopped fresh mint
75ml/5 tbsp chopped fresh parsley
15ml/1 tbsp chopped fresh coriander
2 medium tomatoes, skinned and
    chopped
juice of 1 lemon
75ml/5 tbsp olive oil
salt and black pepper
fresh mint sprigs, to garnish

1 Place the bulgur wheat in a bowl, pour on enough boiling water to cover and leave to soak for 20 minutes.

2 After soaking, place the bulgur wheat in a large sieve and drain thoroughly. Transfer to a bowl.

3 Stir in the spring onions, herbs, tomatoes, lemon juice, olive oil and seasoning. Mix well and chill for about an hour. Garnish with mint.

INDIAN PILAU RICE

INGREDIENTS

Serves 4

225g/8oz/1¼ cups basmati rice, rinsed
    well
1 small onion, finely chopped
1 garlic clove, crushed
30ml/2 tbsp vegetable oil
5ml/1 tsp fennel seeds
15ml/1 tbsp sesame seeds
2.5ml/½ tsp ground turmeric
5ml/1 tsp ground cumin
1.25ml/¼ tsp salt
2 whole cloves
4 cardamom pods, lightly crushed
5 black peppercorns
450ml/¾ pint/1⅞ cups chicken stock
15ml/1 tbsp ground almonds
fresh coriander sprigs, to garnish

1 Soak the rice in water for 30 minutes. Heat the oil in a saucepan, add the onions and garlic, and fry gently for 5–6 minutes, until softened.

2 Stir in the fennel and sesame seeds, the turmeric, cumin, salt, cloves, cardamom pods and peppercorns and fry for about a minute. Drain the rice well, add to the pan and stir-fry for a further 3 minutes.

3 Pour on the chicken stock. Bring to the boil, then cover, reduce the heat to very low and simmer gently for 20 minutes, without removing the lid, until all the liquid has been absorbed.

4 Remove from the heat and leave to stand for 2–3 minutes. Fork up the rice and stir in the ground almonds. Garnish with coriander sprigs.

THAI FRIED NOODLES

INGREDIENTS

Serves 4

225g/8oz thread egg noodles
60ml/4 tbsp vegetable oil
2 garlic cloves, finely chopped
175g/6oz pork tenderloin, sliced into
    thin strips
1 skinless boned chicken breast (about
    175g/6oz), sliced into thin strips
115g/4oz/1 cup cooked peeled shrimps
    (rinsed if canned)
45ml/3 tbsp lime or lemon juice
45ml/3 tbsp oriental fish sauce
30ml/2 tbsp soft light brown sugar
2 eggs, beaten
½ red chilli, seeded and finely chopped
50g/2oz/¾ cup beansprouts
60ml/4 tbsp roasted peanuts, chopped
3 spring onions, cut into 5cm/2in
    lengths and shredded
45ml/3 tbsp chopped fresh coriander

1 Place the noodles in a large pan of boiling water and leave to stand for about 5 minutes.

2 Meanwhile, heat 45ml/3 tbsp of the oil in a wok or large frying pan, add the garlic and cook for 30 seconds. Add the pork and chicken and stir-fry on a high heat until lightly browned, then add the shrimps and stir-fry for 2 minutes.

3 Add the lime or lemon juice, fish sauce and sugar and stir-fry until the sugar has dissolved.

4 Drain the noodles and add to the pan with the remaining 15ml/1 tbsp oil. Toss all the ingredients together.

5 Pour on the beaten eggs. Stir-fry until almost set, then add the chilli and beansprouts. Divide the peanuts, spring onions and coriander leaves into two and add half to the pan. Stir-fry for 2 minutes, then tip on to a serving platter. Sprinkle on the remaining peanuts, spring onions and coriander and serve at once.

VEGETABLES AND SALADS

Nowadays, vegetables are taking centre-stage on menus all over the world, and this chapter demonstrates just how versatile and delicious they can be. The hearty Salade Niçoise, delicious Ratatouille stewed in fruity olive oil, and Mixed Pepper Salad are all from the shores of the Mediterranean. From the Far East, Chinese Crispy Seaweed topped with sweetened almonds is easy to make, and from America hails the crunchy Caesar Salad, packed with crisp croûtons and garlic. Add a touch of zing to potatoes – serve Bombay Spiced Potatoes, or the fiery Spanish Chilli Potatoes – or, if you have a sweeter tooth, try Candied Sweet Potatoes with Bacon. For the ideal accompaniment to a main course, choose from delicious, creamy Leek and Parsnip Purée, Mexican Re-fried Beans, and Chinese Vegetable Stir-fry.

SALADE NIÇOISE

Serves 4

90ml/6 tbsp olive oil
30ml/2 tbsp tarragon vinegar
5ml/1 tsp tarragon or Dijon mustard
1 small garlic clove, crushed
115g/4oz/1 cup French beans
12 small new or salad potatoes
3–4 Little Gem lettuces, roughly
 chopped
200g/7oz can tuna in oil, drained
6 anchovy fillets, halved lengthways
12 black olives, stoned
4 tomatoes, chopped
4 spring onions, finely chopped
10ml/2 tsp capers
30ml/2 tbsp pine nuts
2 hard-boiled eggs, chopped
salt and black pepper
crusty bread, to serve

1 Mix the oil, vinegar, mustard, garlic and seasoning with a wooden spoon in the base of a large salad bowl.

2 Cook the French beans and potatoes in separate pans of boiling salted water until just tender. Drain and add to the bowl with the lettuce, tuna, anchovies, olives, tomatoes, spring onions and capers.

3 Just before serving toast the pine nuts in a small frying pan until lightly browned.

4 Sprinkle over the salad while still hot, add the eggs and toss all the ingredients together well. Serve with chunks of hot crusty bread.

COOK'S TIP
Look out for waxy salad potatoes like Charlotte, Belle de Fontenay or Pink Fir Apple – or simply use new season Jersey Royals.

CAESAR SALAD

For this famous salad, created by the Tijuanan chef called Caesar Cardini in the 1920s, the dressing is traditionally tossed into crunchy Cos lettuce, but any crisp lettuce will do.

INGREDIENTS

Serves 4
1 large cos lettuce
4 thick slices white or Granary bread
   without crusts, cubed
45ml/3 tbsp olive oil
1 garlic clove, crushed

For the dressing
1 egg
1 garlic clove, chopped
30ml/2 tbsp lemon juice
dash of Worcestershire sauce
3 anchovy fillets, chopped
120ml/4fl oz/½ cup olive oil
25g/1oz/5 tbsp grated Parmesan
   cheese
salt and black pepper

1 Preheat the oven to 220°C/425°F/ Gas 7. Separate, rinse and dry the lettuce leaves. Tear the outer leaves roughly and chop the heart. Arrange the lettuce in a large salad bowl.

2 Mix together the cubed bread, olive oil and garlic in a separate bowl until the bread has soaked up the oil. Lay the bread cubes on a baking sheet and place in the oven for about 6–8 minutes (keeping an eye on them) until golden. Remove and leave to cool.

3 To make the dressing, break the egg into the bowl of a food processor or blender and add the garlic, lemon juice, Worcestershire sauce and one of the anchovy fillets. Blend until smooth.

4 With the motor running, pour in the olive oil in a thin stream until the dressing has the consistency of single cream. Season with black pepper and a little salt if needed.

5 Pour the dressing over the salad leaves and toss well, then toss in the garlic croûtons, Parmesan cheese and the remaining anchovies and serve.

CHINESE VEGETABLE STIR-FRY

A typical stir-fried vegetable dish popular all over China. Chinese leaves are like a cross between a cabbage and a crunchy lettuce, with a delicious peppery flavour.

INGREDIENTS

Serves 4
45ml/3 tbsp sunflower oil
15ml/1 tbsp sesame oil
1 garlic clove, chopped
225g/8oz/2 cups broccoli florets, cut into small pieces
115g/4oz/1 cup sugar snap peas
1 whole Chinese leaf (about 450g/1lb) or Savoy cabbage, sliced
4 spring onions, finely chopped
30ml/2 tbsp soy sauce
30ml/2 tbsp dry sherry
15ml/1 tbsp sesame seeds, lightly toasted

1 Heat the oils in a wok or large frying pan until really hot, add the garlic and stir-fry for 30 seconds.

2 Add the broccoli florets and stir-fry for 3 minutes. Add the sugar snap peas and cook for 2 minutes, then toss in the Chinese leaves or cabbage and the spring onions and stir-fry for a further 2 minutes.

3 Pour on the soy sauce, sherry and 30–45ml/2–3 tbsp water and stir-fry for a further 4 minutes, or until the vegetables are just tender. Sprinkle with the toasted sesame seeds and serve hot.

MEDITERREAN MIXED PEPPER SALAD

INGREDIENTS

Serves 4
2 red peppers, halved and seeded
2 yellow peppers, halved and seeded
150ml/¼ pint/⅔ cup olive oil
1 onion, thinly sliced
2 garlic cloves, crushed
squeeze of lemon juice
chopped fresh parsley, to garnish

1 Grill the pepper halves for about 5 minutes, until the skin has blistered and blackened. Pop them into a polythene bag, seal and leave for 5 minutes.

2 Meanwhile, heat 30ml/2 tbsp of the olive oil in a frying pan and add the onion. Fry for about 5–6 minutes, until softened and translucent. Remove from the heat and reserve.

3 Take the peppers out of the bag and peel off the skins. Discard the pepper skins and slice each pepper half into fairly thin strips.

4 Place the peppers, cooked onions and any oil from the pan into a bowl. Add the crushed garlic and pour on the remaining olive oil, add a good squeeze of lemon juice and season. Mix well, cover and marinate for 2–3 hours, stirring the mixture once or twice.

5 Garnish the pepper salad with chopped fresh parsley and serve either as a tasty starter or as an accompaniment to cold meats.

GREEK SPINACH AND CHEESE PIES

INGREDIENTS

Makes 4
15ml/1 tbsp olive oil
1 small onion, finely chopped
275g/10oz fresh spinach, stalks removed
50g/2oz/4 tbsp butter, melted
4 sheets of filo pastry (about 45 x
    25cm/18 x 10in)
1 egg
a good pinch of grated nutmeg
75g/3oz/¾ cup, crumbled Feta cheese
15ml/1 tbsp grated Parmesan cheese
salt and black pepper

1 Preheat the oven to 190°C/375°F/ Gas 5. Heat the oil in a pan, add the onion and fry gently for 5–6 minutes, until softened.

2 Add the spinach leaves and cook, stirring, until the spinach has wilted and some of the liquid evaporated. Leave to cool.

3 Brush four 10cm/4in diameter loose-based tartlet tins with a little melted butter. Take two sheets of the filo pastry and cut each into eight 11cm/4½in squares. Keep the remaining sheets covered.

4 Brush four squares at a time with melted butter. Line the first tartlet tin with one square, gently easing it into the base and up the sides. Leave the edges overhanging.

5 Lay the remaining three buttered squares on top of the first, turning them so the corners form a star shape. Repeat for the remaining tartlet tins.

6 Beat the egg with the nutmeg and seasoning, then stir in the cheeses and spinach. Divide the mixture between the tins and level smooth. Fold the over- hanging pastry back over the filling.

7 Cut one of the remaining sheets of pastry into eight 10cm/4in rounds. Brush with butter and place two on top of each tartlet. Press around the edges to seal. Brush the remaining sheet of pastry with butter and cut into strips. Gently twist each strip and lay on top of the tartlets. Leave to stand for 5 minutes, then bake for about 30–35 minutes, until golden. Serve hot or cold.

COURGETTE AND TOMATO BAKE

A *tian* is a heavy earthenware dish that many French vegetable dishes are cooked in. This typical peasant recipe is just one example.

INGREDIENTS

Serves 4

45ml/3 tbsp olive oil
1 onion, chopped
1 garlic clove, crushed
3 rashers lean bacon, chopped
4 courgettes, grated
2 tomatoes, skinned, seeded and chopped
115g/4oz/1 cup cooked long grain rice
10ml/2 tsp chopped fresh thyme
15ml/1 tbsp chopped fresh parsley
60ml/4 tbsp grated Parmesan cheese
2 eggs, lightly beaten
15ml/1 tbsp fromage frais
salt and black pepper

1 Preheat the oven to 180°C/350°F/ Gas 4. Grease a shallow ovenproof dish with a little olive oil.

2 Heat the oil in a frying pan, add the onion and garlic and fry for 5 minutes until softened.

3 Add the bacon and fry for 2 minutes, then stir in the courgettes and fry for a further 8 minutes, stirring occasionally and letting some of the liquid evaporate. Remove from the heat.

4 Add the tomatoes, rice, herbs, 30ml/2 tbsp of the Parmesan cheese, the eggs, fromage frais and seasoning and mix well.

5 Spoon the courgette mixture into the dish and sprinkle over the remaining 30ml/2 tbsp of Parmesan cheese. Bake for 45 minutes, until set and golden. Serve hot.

COOK'S TIP
For a dinner party, divide the mixture among lightly greased individual gratin dishes and bake for about 25 minutes until set and golden.

MEXICAN RE-FRIED BEANS

In Mexico beans are served at every meal. In this recipe for *frijoles refritos* the beans are cooked once and then re-fried for extra flavour.

INGREDIENTS

Serves 4
30ml/2 tbsp sunflower oil
1 onion, diced
1 garlic clove, crushed
2 x 400g/14oz cans red kidney beans
1 fresh green chilli, seeded and diced
salt and black pepper

For re-frying the beans
45ml/3 tbsp vegetable oil
1 small onion, diced
1 whole green chilli, seeded and diced
natural yogurt, chopped spring onion
*   and chilli powder, to garnish*

1 Heat the oil in a pan and add the onion and garlic. Fry for 5–6 minutes, until the onions have softened and lightly browned.

2 Stir in the beans with the liquid from the cans, add the chilli and a good pinch of salt. Bring to the boil, then cover and simmer gently for 45 minutes. Mash roughly with a potato masher and stir until thickened to a porridge consistency. Leave to cool.

3 To re-fry the beans, heat about 45ml/3 tbsp of oil in a pan and add the onion and chilli. Fry for 5 minutes, then stir in the beans, pressing them down with the back of a spoon as they fry and then stirring so they don't burn. Repeat for about 5 minutes, until heated through, then season lightly.

4 Serve the beans topped with a spoonful of yogurt and a sprinkling of spring onions and chilli powder.

COOK'S TIP
The beans are delicious with lamb or pork chops, roast red meats, spicy sausages, or as a toast topper with shredded lettuce and soured cream.

SPANISH GREEN BEANS WITH HAM

Judias verdes con jamón are green beans cooked with a Spanish raw-cured dried Serrano ham – use Parma ham or unsmoked bacon as alternatives.

INGREDIENTS

Serves 4
450g/1lb French beans
45ml/3 tbsp olive oil
1 onion, thinly sliced
2 garlic cloves, finely chopped
75g/3oz Parma ham or bacon,
*   chopped*
salt and black pepper

1 Cook the beans in boiling salted water for about 5–6 minutes, until just tender but still with a bit of bite.

2 Meanwhile, heat the oil in a pan, add the onions and fry for 5 minutes, until softened and translucent. Add the garlic and ham and cook for a further minute or two.

3 Drain the beans add to the pan and cook, stirring occasionally, for 2–3 minutes. Season well and serve hot.

CANDIED SWEET POTATOES WITH BACON

This sweet potato dish is always served for Thanksgiving in North America to celebrate the settlers' first harvest.

INGREDIENTS

Serves 4
2 large sweet potatoes (450g/1lb each), washed
50g/2oz/½ cup soft light brown sugar
30ml/2 tbsp lemon juice
40g/1½oz/3 tbsp butter
4 rashers smoked streaky bacon, cut into thin strips
salt and black pepper
sprig of flat leaf parsley, to garnish

1 Preheat the oven to 190°C/375°F/ Gas 5 and lightly butter a shallow ovenproof dish. Cut the unpeeled potatoes crossways into four and place the pieces in a pan of boiling water. Cover and cook for about 25 minutes, until just tender.

2 Drain and when cool enough to handle, peel and slice quite thickly. Arrange in a single layer, overlapping, in the prepared dish.

3 Sprinkle over the sugar and lemon juice and dot with butter. Top with the bacon and season well.

4 Bake uncovered for 35–40 minutes, basting once or twice, until the potatoes are tender.

5 Preheat the grill to a high heat. Grill the potatoes for 2–3 minutes, until they are browned and the bacon crispy. Serve hot, garnished with parsley.

RATATOUILLE

INGREDIENTS

Serves 4

2 large aubergines, roughly chopped
4 courgettes, roughly chopped
150ml/¼ pint/⅔ cup olive oil
2 onions, sliced
2 garlic cloves, chopped
1 large red pepper, seeded and roughly
  chopped
2 large yellow peppers, seeded and
  roughly chopped
fresh rosemary sprig
fresh thyme sprig
5ml/1 tsp coriander seeds, crushed
3 plum tomatoes, skinned, seeded and
  chopped
8 basil leaves, torn
salt and black pepper
fresh parsley or basil sprigs,
  to garnish

1 Sprinkle the aubergines and courgettes with salt, then put them in a colander with a plate and weight on top to extract the bitter juices. Leave for about 30 minutes.

2 Heat the olive oil in a large saucepan. Add the onions, fry gently for about 6–7 minutes, until just softened, then add the garlic and cook for another 2 minutes.

3 Rinse the aubergines and courgettes and pat dry with kitchen paper. Add to the pan with the peppers, increase the heat and sauté until the peppers are just turning brown.

4 Add the herbs and coriander seeds, then cover the pan and cook gently for about 40 minutes.

5 Add the tomatoes and season well. Cook gently for a further 10 minutes, until the vegetables are soft but not too mushy. Remove the sprigs of herbs. Stir in the torn basil leaves and check the seasoning. Leave to cool slightly and serve warm or cold, garnished with sprigs of parsley or basil.

BOMBAY SPICED POTATOES

This Indian potato dish uses a mixture of whole and ground spices. Look out for mustard and black onion seeds in specialist food shops.

─────── INGREDIENTS ───────

Serves 4

4 large potatoes (Maris Piper or King
 Edward), cubed
60ml/4 tbsp sunflower oil
1 garlic clove, finely chopped
10ml/2 tsp brown mustard seeds
5ml/1 tsp black onion seeds (optional)
5ml/1 tsp ground turmeric
5ml/1 tsp ground cumin
5ml/1 tsp ground coriander
5ml/1 tsp fennel seeds
salt and black pepper
a good squeeze of lemon juice
chopped fresh coriander and lemon
 wedges, to garnish

1 Bring a pan of salted water to the boil, add the potatoes and simmer for about 4 minutes, until just tender. Drain well.

2 Heat the oil in a large frying pan and add the garlic along with all the whole and ground spices. Fry gently for 1–2 minutes, stirring until the mustard seeds start to pop.

3 Add the potatoes and stir-fry on a moderate heat for about 5 minutes, until heated through and well coated with the spicy oil.

4 Season well and sprinkle over the lemon juice. Garnish with chopped coriander and lemon wedges. Serve as an accompaniment to curries or other strong flavoured meat dishes.

SPANISH CHILLI POTATOES

The name of this Spanish *tapas* dish, *Patatas Bravas*, means fierce, hot potatoes. You can always reduce the amount of chilli to suit your taste.

─────── INGREDIENTS ───────

Serves 4

1kg/2lb new or salad potatoes
60ml/4 tbsp olive oil
1 onion, finely chopped
2 garlic cloves, crushed
15ml/1 tbsp tomato purée
200g/7oz can chopped tomatoes
15ml/1 tbsp red wine vinegar
2–3 small dried red chillies, seeded and
 chopped finely, or 5–10ml/1–2 tsp
 hot chilli powder
5ml/1 tsp paprika
salt and black pepper
fresh flat leaf parsley sprig, to garnish

1 Boil the potatoes in their skins for 10–12 minutes or until just tender. Drain well and leave to cool, then cut in half and reserve.

2 Heat the oil in a large pan and add the onions and garlic. Fry gently for 5–6 minutes, until just softened. Stir in the tomato purée, tomatoes, vinegar, chilli and paprika and simmer for about 5 minutes.

3 Add the potatoes and mix into the sauce mixture until well coated. Cover and simmer gently for about 8–10 minutes, or until the potatoes are tender. Season well and transfer to a warmed serving dish. Serve garnished with a sprig of flat leaf parsley.

CHINESE CRISPY SEAWEED

In northern China they use a special kind of seaweed for this dish, but spring greens, shredded very finely, make a very good alternative. Serve either as a starter or as an accompaniment to a Chinese meal.

INGREDIENTS

Serves 4
225g/8oz spring greens
groundnut or corn oil, for deep-frying
1.25ml/¼ tsp salt
10ml/2 tsp soft light brown sugar
30–45ml/2–3 tbsp toasted, flaked
  almonds

1 Cut out and discard any tough stalks from the spring greens. Place about six leaves on top of each other and roll up into a tight roll.

2 Using a sharp knife, slice across into thin shreds. Lay on a tray and leave to dry for about 2 hours.

3 Heat about 5–7.5cm/2–3in of oil in a wok or pan to 190°C/375°F. Carefully place a handful of the leaves into the oil – it will bubble and spit for the first 10 seconds and then die down. Deep-fry for about 45 seconds, or until a slightly darker green – do not to let the leaves burn.

4 Remove with a slotted spoon, drain on kitchen paper and transfer to a serving dish. Keep warm in the oven while frying the remainder.

5 When you have fried all the shredded leaves, sprinkle with the salt and sugar and toss lightly. Garnish with the toasted almonds.

COOK'S TIP
Make sure that your deep-frying pan is deep enough to allow the oil to bubble up during cooking. The pan should be less than half full.

LEEK AND PARSNIP PURÉE

Vegetable purées are popular in Britain and France served with meat, chicken or fish dishes. This mixture of leeks and parsnips makes a tasty accompaniment.

INGREDIENTS

Serves 4
2 large leeks, sliced
3 medium parsnips, sliced
knob of butter
45ml/3 tbsp top of the milk
30ml/2 tbsp fromage frais
a good squeeze of lemon juice
salt and black pepper
a good pinch of grated nutmeg to
  garnish

1 Steam or boil the leeks and parsnips together for about 15 minutes, until tender. Drain well, then place in a food processor or blender.

2 Add the remaining ingredients to the processor or blender. Whizz until really smooth, then check the seasoning. Transfer to a warmed bowl and garnish with a sprinkling of nutmeg.

HOT PUDDINGS

Hot, steaming and delicious, here are puddings to warm up those chilly winter months or just to add the perfect finale to any meal. Favourite American classics are the Spiced Pumpkin Pie, and Creole Bread and Butter Pudding served with an irresistible hot whisky cream sauce. British favourites include Lemon Meringue Pie, and an Apple and Blackberry Nut Crumble that all purple-fingered blackberry-pickers would be proud of. From France come a bubbling pan of Crêpes Suzette, and a classic caramelized Upside-down Apple Tart – both dinner-party winners. Thai Fried Bananas make a delicious last-minute sweet and, if it's nursery puddings you crave, try the steamed Austrian Nut Pudding with lashings of raspberry sauce.

AMERICAN SPICED PUMPKIN PIE

INGREDIENTS

Serves 4-6

175g/6oz/1½ cups plain flour
pinch of salt
75g/3oz/6 tbsp unsalted butter
15ml/1 tbsp caster sugar
450g/1lb/4 cups peeled fresh pumpkin,
*   cubed, or 400g/14oz/2 cups canned*
*   pumpkin, drained*
115g/4oz/⅝ cup soft light brown sugar
1.25ml/¼ tsp salt
1.25ml/¼ tsp ground allspice
2.5ml/½ tsp ground cinnamon
2.5ml/½ tsp ground ginger
2 eggs, lightly beaten
120ml/4fl oz/½ cup double cream
whipped cream, to serve

1 Place the flour in a bowl with the salt and butter and rub in with your fingertips until the mixture resembles breadcrumbs (or use a food processor).

2 Stir in the sugar and add about 30–45ml/2–3 tbsp water and mix to a soft dough. Knead the dough lightly on a floured surface. Flatten out into a round, wrap in a polythene bag and chill for about 1 hour.

3 Preheat the oven to 200°C/400°F/ Gas 6 with a baking sheet inside. If you are using raw pumpkin for the pie, steam for 15 minutes until quite tender, then leave to cool completely. Purée the steamed or canned pumpkin in a food processor or blender until very smooth.

4 Roll out the pastry quite thinly and use to line a 23.5cm/9½in (measured across the top) x 2.5cm/1in deep pie tin. Trim off any excess pastry and reserve for the decoration. Prick the base of the pastry case with a fork.

5 Cut as many leaf shapes as you can from the excess pastry and make vein markings with the back of a knife on each. Brush the edge of the pastry with water and stick the leaves all round the edge. Chill.

6 In a bowl mix together the pumpkin purée, sugar, salt, spices, eggs and cream and pour into the pastry case.

7 Place on the preheated baking sheet and bake for 15 minutes. Then reduce the temperature to 180°C/ 350°F/Gas 4 and cook for a further 30 minutes, or until the filling is set and the pastry golden. Serve the pie warm with whipped cream.

LEMON MERINGUE PIE

Makes an 18.5cm/7½in pie
115g/4oz/1 cup plain flour
50g/2oz/4 tbsp butter, cubed
25g/1oz/3 tbsp ground almonds
25g/1oz/2 tbsp caster sugar
1 egg yolk

For the filling
juice of 3 lemons
finely grated rind of 2 lemons
45ml/3 tbsp cornflour
75g/3oz/6 tbsp caster sugar
2 egg yolks
15ml/1 tbsp butter

For the meringue
2 egg whites
115g/4oz/½ cup caster sugar

1 To make the pastry, sift the flour into a bowl, add the butter and rub in with your fingertips until the mixture resembles breadcrumbs (or use a food processor). Stir in the almonds and sugar, add the egg yolk and 30ml/ 2 tbsp cold water. Mix with your hands until the pastry comes together.

2 Knead lightly on a floured surface then wrap and chill for about 30 minutes. Meanwhile, preheat the oven to 200°C/400°F/Gas 6 and pop in a baking sheet to heat up.

3 Roll out the pastry to a 20cm/8in round and use it to line a 18.5cm/ 7½in fluted loose-based flan tin. Prick the base with a fork. Line with grease-proof paper and fill with baking beans.

4 Place the tin on the preheated baking sheet and bake blind for 12 minutes. Remove the paper and beans and bake for a further 5 minutes. Remove from the oven and cool. Reduce the temperature to 150°C/300°F/Gas 2.

5 To make the filling, put the lemon juice and rind into a jug (you should have 150ml/ ¼ pint/⅔ cup). Blend the cornflour with a little of the lemon juice, then gradually stir in the rest. Pour into a saucepan and add 150ml/ ¼ pint/⅔ cup water.

6 Bring slowly to the boil, stirring until smooth and thickened. Remove from the heat and beat in the sugar and egg yolks, then add the butter. Spoon into the pastry case.

7 To make the meringue, whisk the egg whites until stiff, then gradually whisk in the sugar a tablespoon at a time until thick and glossy. Pile the meringue on top of the lemon filling, spreading and swirling it with the back of a spoon. Bake for 30–35 minutes, or until the meringue is golden and crisp.

ZABAGLIONE

A much-loved simple Italian pudding traditionally made with Marsala, an Italian fortified wine. Madeira is a good alternative.

─────── INGREDIENTS ───────

Serves 4
4 egg yolks
50g/2oz/4 tbsp caster sugar
60ml/4 tbsp Marsala or Madeira wine
Amaretti biscuits, to serve

1 Place the egg yolks and sugar in a large heatproof bowl and whisk with an electric whisk until the mixture is pale and thick.

2 Gradually add the Marsala or Madeira, whisking well after each addition (at this stage the mixture will be quite runny).

3 Now place the bowl over a pan of gently simmering water and continue to whisk for at least 5–7 minutes, until the mixture becomes thick and mousse-like; when the beaters are lifted they should leave a thick trail on the surface of the mixture. (If you don't beat the mixture for long enough, the zabaglione will be too runny and will probably separate.)

4 Pour into four warmed, stemmed glasses and serve immediately with the Amaretti biscuits for dipping.

COOK'S TIP
If you don't have any Marsala or Madeira you could use a medium sweet sherry or a dessert wine.

MIXED BERRY SOUFFLÉ OMELETTE

These light French omelettes take only a few minutes to cook and are best eaten straight away.

─────── INGREDIENTS ───────

Makes 2 (serves 4)
4 eggs, separated
finely grated rind of 1 lemon
25g/1oz/2 tbsp caster sugar
drop of vanilla essence
15ml/1 tbsp single cream
25g/1oz/2 tbsp butter
60ml/4 tbsp mixed berry conserve,
  warmed
icing sugar, for dusting
30ml/2 tbsp toasted flaked almonds,
  and fresh mint sprigs to decorate

1 Place the egg yolks in a bowl and add the lemon rind, sugar, vanilla essence and cream. Beat with an electric or balloon whisk until pale and slightly thickened, then set aside.

2 Whisk the egg whites in a separate bowl until holding stiff peaks. Gently beat 30ml/2 tbsp of the whisked whites into the egg yolk mixture to loosen it, then fold in the remainder using a large metal spoon.

3 Melt half the butter in a 23cm/9in frying pan and pour on half the egg mixture. Cook on a gentle heat for about 4 minutes, or until just set and lightly golden underneath.

4 Pop the pan under the hot grill, for about 30 seconds, keeping a close eye on it until just browned. Remove from the grill, and spoon half the warmed conserve over the omelette. Fold the omelette in half and slide it on to a warmed plate.

5 Dust with a little icing sugar, sprinkle with half the almonds and decorate with mint. Cut in half and share between two people. Use remaining mixture to make a second omelette.

CRÊPES SUZETTE

Makes 8
115g/4oz/1 cup plain flour
pinch of salt
1 egg
1 egg yolk
*300ml/½ pint/1¼ cups semi-skimmed
milk*
*15g/½oz/1 tbsp butter, melted, plus
extra, for frying*

For the sauce
2 large oranges
50g/2oz/4 tbsp butter
*50g/2oz/½ cup soft light brown
sugar*
15ml/1 tbsp Grand Marnier
15ml/1 tbsp brandy

1 Sift the flour and salt into a bowl and make a well in the centre. Crack the egg and extra yolk into the well.

2 Stir the eggs with a wooden spoon to incorporate the flour from round the edges. When the mixture thickens, gradually pour on the milk, beating well after each addition, until a smooth batter is formed.

3 Stir in the butter, transfer to a jug, cover and chill for 30 minutes.

4 Heat a medium (about 20cm/8in) shallow frying pan, add a little butter and heat until sizzling. Pour on a little of the batter, tilting the pan back and forth to cover the base thinly.

5 Cook over a medium heat for 1–2 minutes until lightly browned underneath, then flip over using a palette knife and cook for a further minute. Repeat this process until you have eight crêpes. Stack them up on a plate, as they are ready.

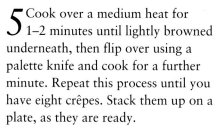

6 Using a zester, pare the rind from one of the oranges and reserve about a teaspoon for decoration. Squeeze the juice from both oranges and set aside.

7 To make the sauce, melt the butter in a large frying pan and add the sugar with the orange rind and juice. Heat gently until the sugar has dissolved and the mixture is gently bubbling. Fold each crêpe in quarters. Add to the pan one at a time, coating them in the sauce and folding each one in half again. Gently move to the side of the pan to make room for the others.

8 Pour on the Grand Marnier and brandy and cook gently for 2–3 minutes, until the sauce has slightly caramelized. (For that extra touch, flame the brandy as you pour it into the pan.) Sprinkle with the reserved orange rind and serve straight from the pan.

CREOLE BREAD AND BUTTER PUDDING

INGREDIENTS

Serves 4-6

4 ready-to-eat dried apricots, chopped
15ml/1 tbsp raisins
30ml/2 tbsp sultanas
15ml/1 tbsp chopped mixed peel
1 French loaf (about 200g/7oz), thinly sliced
50g/2oz/4 tbsp butter, melted
450ml/¾ pint/1⅞ cups milk
150ml/¼ pint/⅔ cup double cream
115g/4oz/½ cup caster sugar
3 eggs
2.5ml/½ tsp vanilla essence
30ml/2 tbsp whisky

For the cream

150ml/¼ pint/⅔ cup double cream
30ml/2 tbsp Greek-style yogurt
15–30ml/1–2 tbsp whisky
15ml/1 tbsp caster sugar

1 Preheat the oven to 180°C/350°F/ Gas 4. Lightly grease a deep 1.5–1.75 litre/2½ pint/6 cup ovenproof dish with butter. Mix together the dried fruits and sprinkle a little over the base of the dish. Brush both sides of the bread slices with melted butter.

2 Fill the dish with alternate layers of bread slices and dried fruit, finishing with a layer of bread.

3 Heat the milk and cream together in a pan until just boiling. Meanwhile, place the sugar, eggs and vanilla essence in a bowl and whisk together.

4 Whisk the hot milk and cream into the eggs and then strain over the bread and fruit. Sprinkle the whisky over the top. Press the bread into the milk and egg mixture, cover with foil and leave to stand for 20 minutes.

5 Place the dish in a roasting tin half filled with water and bake for about 1 hour or until the custard is just set. Remove the foil and return the pudding to the oven to cook for a further 10 minutes, until the bread is golden.

6 Just before serving, place the cream, Greek yogurt, whisky and sugar into a small pan, stir and heat gently. Serve with the hot pudding.

ORANGE RICE PUDDING

In Spain, Greece, Italy and Morocco rice puddings are a favourite dish, especially when sweetened with honey and flavoured with orange.

INGREDIENTS

Serves 4

50g/2oz/4 tbsp short-grain pudding rice
600ml/1 pint/2½ cups milk
30–45ml/2–3 tbsp clear honey (according to taste)
finely grated rind of ½ small orange
150ml/¼ pint/⅔ cup double cream
15ml/1 tbsp chopped pistachio nuts, toasted

1 Mix the rice with the milk, honey and orange rind in a saucepan and bring to the boil, then reduce the heat, cover and simmer very gently for about 1¼ hours, stirring regularly.

2 Remove the lid and continue cooking and stirring for about 15–20 minutes, until the rice is creamy.

3 Pour in the cream and simmer for 5–8 minutes longer. Serve the rice sprinkled with the pistachio nuts in individual warmed bowls.

APPLE AND BLACKBERRY NUT CRUMBLE

This much-loved dish of Bramley apples and blackberries topped with a golden, sweet crumble is perhaps one of the simplest and most delicious of British hot puddings.

INGREDIENTS

Serves 4

1kg/2lb (4 medium) Bramley apples, peeled, cored and sliced
115g/4oz/½ cup butter, cubed
115g/4oz/⅝ cup soft light brown sugar
175g/6oz/1¾ cups blackberries
75g/3oz/¾ cup wholemeal flour
75g/3oz/¾ cup plain flour
2.5ml/½ tsp ground cinnamon
45ml/3 tbsp chopped mixed nuts, toasted
custard, cream or ice cream, to serve

1 Preheat the oven to 180°C/350°F/ Gas 4. Lightly butter a 1.2 litre/ 2 pint/5 cup ovenproof dish.

2 Place the apples in a pan with 25g/1oz/2 tbsp of the butter, 25g/1oz/2 tbsp of the sugar and 15ml/ 1 tbsp water. Cover and cook gently for about 10 minutes, until just tender but still holding their shape.

3 Remove from the heat and gently stir in the blackberries. Spoon the mixture into the ovenproof dish and set aside while you make the topping.

4 To make the crumble topping, sift the flours and cinnamon into a bowl (tip in any of the bran left in the sieve). Add the remaining 75g/3oz/ 6 tbsp butter and rub into the flour with your fingertips until the mixture resembles fine breadcrumbs (or you can use a food processor).

5 Stir in the remaining 75g/3oz/6 tbsp sugar and the nuts and mix well. Sprinkle the crumble topping over the fruit. Bake for 35–40 minutes, until the top is golden brown. Serve hot with custard, cream or ice cream.

AUSTRIAN NUT PUDDING

Serves 4
butter, for greasing
50g/2oz/4 tbsp caster sugar, plus
a little extra for sprinkling
115g/4oz/1 cup chopped hazelnuts
50g/2oz/4 tbsp butter, softened
2 eggs, separated
25g/1oz/½ cup very fine fresh white
breadcrumbs
175g/6oz/1¼ cups fresh raspberries
icing sugar, to taste
cream, to serve

1 Preheat the oven to 160°C/325°F/
Gas 3. Lightly butter a 900ml/1½
pint/3¾ cup pudding basin and sprinkle
with a little caster sugar.

2 Spread the hazelnuts on to a baking
sheet and bake for 15–20 minutes,
until toasted and golden. Remove from
the oven and leave to cool.

3 Meanwhile, place the butter and
sugar in a bowl and beat until pale
and creamy. Beat in the egg yolks.

4 Process the cooled nuts in a food
processor until finely ground.

5 Mix 15ml/1 tbsp water into the
breadcrumbs and beat into the
creamed mixture with the hazelnuts.

6 Place the egg whites in a clean bowl
and whisk until stiff. Beat about
30ml/2 tbsp into the creamed mixture
to loosen it slightly and carefully fold in
the remainder with a metal spoon.

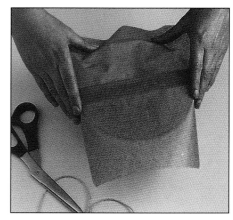

7 Spoon into the prepared basin and
top with a circle of greaseproof
paper with a fold in it, secured tightly
with string. Cover with foil and steam
for 1½ hours, checking and topping up
the water level if it needs it.

8 Meanwhile, press the raspberries
through a sieve into a bowl and add
icing sugar to sweeten. When the pudding is cooked, turn out and serve hot
with the raspberry sauce and cream.

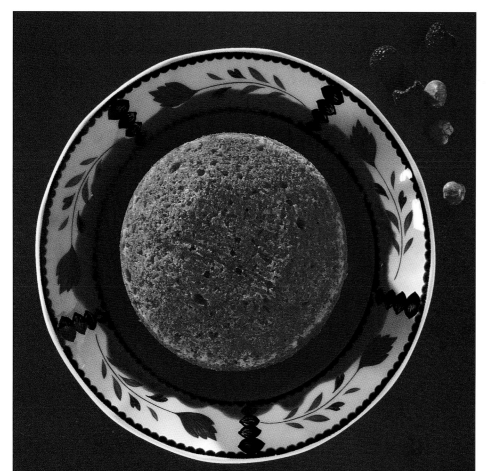

UPSIDE-DOWN APPLE TART

This delicious caramelized fruit tart from France, known as *Tarte Tatin*, was originally created by the Tatin sisters who ran a popular restaurant in Sologne in the Orléanais.

INGREDIENTS

Serves 4
For the pastry
50g/2oz/4 tbsp butter, softened
40g/1½oz/3 tbsp caster sugar
1 egg
115g/4oz/1 cup plain flour
pinch of salt

For the apple layer
75g/3oz/6 tbsp butter, softened
75g/3oz/½ cup soft light brown
  sugar
10 Cox's Pippins apples, peeled, cored
  and thickly sliced
whipped cream, to serve

1 To make the pastry, cream the butter and sugar in a bowl until pale and creamy. Beat in the egg, then sift in the flour and salt and mix to a soft dough. Knead lightly on a floured surface, then wrap and chill for 1 hour.

2 Grease a 23cm/9in cake tin then add 50g/2oz/4 tbsp of the butter. Place the cake tin on the hob and melt the butter gently. Remove and sprinkle over 50g/2oz/⅓ cup of the sugar.

3 Arrange the apple slices on top, then sprinkle with the remaining sugar and dot with the remaining butter.

4 Preheat the oven to 230°C/450°F/ Gas 8. Place the cake tin on the hob again over a low to medium heat for about 15 minutes, until a light golden caramel forms on the bottom. Remove the tin from the heat.

5 Roll out the pastry on a lightly floured surface to a round the same size as the tin and lay on top of the apples. Tuck the pastry edges down round the sides of the apples.

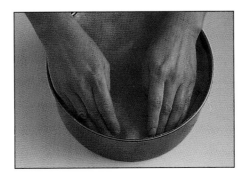

6 Bake for about 20–25 minutes, until the pastry is golden. Remove the tart from the oven and leave to stand for about 5 minutes.

7 Place an upturned plate on top of the tin and holding the two together with a dish towel, turn the apple tart out on to the plate. Serve while still warm with whipped cream.

> **COOK'S TIP**
> Cox's Pippins apples are perfect for this tart because they hold their shape so well. If they are not available, use another firm, sweet eating apple instead.

SPICED MEXICAN FRITTERS

Hot, sweet and spicy fritters are popular in both Spain and Mexico for either breakfast or a mid-morning snack.

INGREDIENTS

Makes 16 (serves 4)
175g/6oz/1¼ cups raspberries
45ml/3 tbsp icing sugar
45ml/3 tbsp orange juice

For the fritters
50g/2oz/4 tbsp butter
65g/2½oz/⅔ cup plain flour, sifted
2 eggs, lightly beaten
15ml/1 tbsp ground almonds
corn oil, for frying
15ml/1 tbsp icing sugar and 2.5ml/
*   ½ tsp ground cinnamon, for dusting*
8 fresh raspberries, to decorate

1 First make the raspberry sauce. Mash the raspberries with the icing sugar and then push through a sieve into a bowl to remove all the seeds. Stir in the orange juice and chill while making the fritters.

2 To make the fritters, place the butter and 150ml/¼ pint/⅔ cup water in a saucepan and heat gently until the butter has melted. Bring to the boil and, when boiling, add the sifted flour all at once and turn off the heat.

3 Beat until the mixture leaves the sides of the pan and forms a ball. Cool slightly then beat in the eggs a little at a time, then add the almonds.

4 Spoon the mixture into a piping bag fitted with a large star nozzle. Half-fill a saucepan or deep-fat fryer with the oil and heat to 190°C/375°F.

5 Pipe about four 5cm/2in lengths at a time into the hot oil, cutting off the raw mixture with a knife as you go. Deep-fry for about 3–4 minutes, turning occasionally, until puffed up and golden. Drain on kitchen paper and keep warm in the oven while frying the remainder.

6 When you have fried all the mixture, dust the hot fritters with icing sugar and cinnamon. Serve three or four per person on serving plates drizzled with a little of the raspberry sauce, dust again with sieved icing sugar and decorate with fresh raspberries.

THAI FRIED BANANAS

A very simple and quick Thai pudding – bananas fried in butter, brown sugar and lime juice, and sprinkled with toasted coconut.

INGREDIENTS

Serves 4
40g/1½oz/3 tbsp butter
4 large slightly underripe bananas
15ml/1 tbsp desiccated coconut
60ml/4 tbsp soft light brown sugar
60ml/4 tbsp lime juice
2 fresh lime slices, to decorate
thick and creamy natural yogurt,
*   to serve*

1 Heat the butter in a large frying pan or wok and fry the bananas for 1–2 minutes on each side, or until they are lightly golden in colour.

2 Meanwhile, dry-fry the coconut in a small frying pan until lightly browned and reserve.

3 Sprinkle the sugar into the pan with the bananas, add the lime juice and cook, stirring until dissolved. Sprinkle the coconut over the bananas, decorate with lime slices and serve with the thick and creamy yogurt.

APPLE STRUDEL

This Austrian pudding is traditionally made with paper-thin layers of buttered strudel pastry, filled with spiced apples and nuts. Ready-made filo pastry makes an easy substitute.

―――――――― INGREDIENTS ――――――――

Serves 4-6

75g/3oz/¾ cup hazelnuts, chopped and
    roasted
30ml/2 tbsp nibbed almonds, roasted
50g/2oz/4 tbsp demerara sugar
2.5ml/½ tsp ground cinnamon
grated rind and juice of ½ lemon
2 large Bramley cooking apples, peeled,
    cored and chopped
50g/2oz/⅓ cup sultanas
4 large sheets filo pastry
50g/2oz/4 tbsp unsalted butter, melted
icing sugar, for dusting
cream, custard or yogurt, to serve

1 Preheat the oven to 190°C/375°F/ Gas 5. In a bowl mix together the hazelnuts, almonds, sugar, cinnamon, lemon rind and juice, apples and sultanas. Set aside.

2 Lay one sheet of filo pastry on a clean dish towel and brush with melted butter. Lay a second sheet on top and brush again with melted butter. Repeat with the remaining two sheets.

3 Spread the fruit and nut mixture over the pastry, leaving a 7.5cm/3in border at each of the shorter ends. Fold the pastry ends in over the filling. Roll up from one long edge to the other, using the dish towel to help.

4 Carefully transfer the strudel to a greased baking sheet, placing the seam side down. Brush all over with butter and bake for 30–35 minutes, until golden and crisp. Dust with icing sugar and serve while still hot with cream, custard or yogurt.

CHOCOLATE FRUIT FONDUE

Fondues originated in Switzerland and this sweet treat is the perfect ending to any meal.

―――――――― INGREDIENTS ――――――――

Serves 6-8

16 fresh strawberries
4 rings fresh pineapple, cut into wedges
2 small nectarines, stoned and cut into
    wedges
1 kiwi fruit, halved and thickly sliced
small bunch of black seedless grapes
2 bananas, chopped
1 small eating apple, cored and cut into
    wedges
lemon juice, for brushing
225g/8oz plain chocolate
15g/½oz/1 tbsp butter
150ml/¼ pint/⅔ cup single cream
45ml/3 tbsp Irish cream liqueur
15ml/1 tbsp pistachio nuts, chopped

1 Arrange the fruit on a serving platter and brush the banana and apple pieces with a little lemon juice. Cover and chill until ready to serve.

2 Place the chocolate, butter, cream and liqueur in a heatproof bowl over a pan of gently simmering water. Stir occasionally until melted and completely smooth.

3 Pour the chocolate mixture into a warmed serving bowl and sprinkle with the pistachios. To serve, guests help themselves by skewering fruits on to fondue forks or dessert forks and dipping in the hot chocolate sauce.

COLD DESSERTS

Perhaps the best thing about cold puddings is that you can make them well in advance and avoid all those last-minute panics! Another wonderful thing is that they taste so good. In this chapter are a selection of international classics, some with new twists but all guaranteed to be easy to make. For instant success, try Chinese Fruit Salad steeped in a lime syrup, a British Rhubarb and Orange Fool, Italian poached apricots, or the Greek Fig and Honey Pudding. For special occasions, the American classic Mississippi Pecan Pie, and Crème Caramel from France are all-time favourites, and the Australian Hazelnut Pavlova is bound to impress the guests. For ice cream fanatics, Rippled Chocolate Ice Cream is unbeatable, but for a change try the flavour of the Far East in the delicious Mango Ice Cream, packed with fruit.

CRÈME CARAMEL

The classic, creamy, caramel-
flavoured custard from France.

INGREDIENTS

Serves 4-6

115g/4oz/½ cup granulated sugar
300ml/½ pint/1¼ cups milk
300ml/½ pint/1¼ cups single cream
6 eggs
75g/3oz/6 tbsp caster sugar
2.5ml/½ tsp vanilla essence

1 Preheat the oven to 150°C/300°F/
Gas 2 and half-fill a large roasting
tin with water.

2 Place the granulated sugar in a
saucepan with 60ml/4 tbsp water
and heat gently, swirling the pan
occasionally, until the sugar has
dissolved. Increase the heat and boil to
a good caramel colour.

3 Immediately pour the caramel into
an ovenproof soufflé dish. Place in
the roasting tin and set aside.

4 To make the egg custard, heat the
milk and cream together in a pan
until almost boiling. Meanwhile, beat
the eggs, caster sugar and vanilla
essence together in a bowl using a large
balloon whisk.

5 Whisk the hot milk into the eggs
and sugar, then strain the liquid
through a sieve into the soufflé dish,
on top of the cooled caramel base.

6 Transfer the tin to the oven and
bake in the centre for about 1½–2
hours (topping up the water level after
1 hour), or until the custard has set in
the centre. Lift the dish carefully out of
the water and leave to cool, then cover
and chill overnight.

7 Loosen the sides of the chilled custard with a knife and then place an
inverted plate (large enough to hold the
caramel sauce that will flow out as
well) on top of the dish. Holding the
dish and plate together, turn upside
down and give the whole thing a quick
shake to release the crème caramel.

AUSTRALIAN HAZELNUT PAVLOVA

INGREDIENTS

Serves 4-6

3 egg whites
175g/6oz/¾ cup caster sugar
5ml/1 tsp cornflour
5ml/1 tsp white wine vinegar
40g/1½oz/5 tbsp chopped roasted
  hazelnuts
250ml/8fl oz/1 cup double cream
15ml/1 tbsp orange juice
30ml/2 tbsp natural thick and creamy
  yogurt
2 ripe nectarines, stoned and sliced
225g/8oz/2 cups raspberries, halved
15–30ml/1–2 tbsp redcurrant jelly,
  warmed

1 Preheat the oven to 140°C/275°F/
Gas 1. Lightly grease a baking sheet.
Draw a 20cm/8in circle on a sheet of
baking parchment. Place pencil-side
down on the baking sheet.

2 Place the egg whites in a clean,
grease-free bowl and whisk with an
electric mixer until stiff. Whisk in the
sugar 15ml/1 tbsp at a time, whisking
well after each addition.

3 Add the cornflour, vinegar and
hazelnuts and fold in carefully with
a large metal spoon.

4 Spoon the meringue on to the
marked circle and spread out to the
edges, making a dip in the centre.

5 Bake for about 1¼–1½ hours, until
crisp. Leave to cool completely and
transfer to a serving platter.

6 Whip the cream and orange juice
until just thick, stir in the yogurt
and spoon on to the meringue. Top
with the fruit and drizzle over the redcurrant jelly. Serve immediately.

CHINESE FRUIT SALAD

For an unusual fruit salad with an oriental flavour, try this mixture of fruits in a tangy lime and lychee syrup topped with a light sprinkling of toasted sesame seeds.

───── INGREDIENTS ─────

Serves 4

115g/4oz/½ cup caster sugar
thinly pared rind and juice of 1 lime
400g/14oz can lychees in syrup
1 ripe mango, stoned and sliced
1 eating apple, cored and sliced
2 bananas, chopped
1 star fruit, sliced (optional)
5ml/1 tsp sesame seeds, toasted

1 Place the sugar in a saucepan with 300ml/½ pint/1¼ cups water and the lime rind. Heat gently until the sugar dissolves, then increase the heat and boil gently for about 7–8 minutes. Remove from the heat and leave on one side to cool.

2 Drain the lychees into a jug and pour the juice into the cooled lime syrup with the lime juice. Place all the prepared fruit in a bowl and pour over the lime and lychee syrup. Chill for about 1 hour. Just before serving, sprinkle with toasted sesame seeds.

APRICOT AND ALMOND JALOUSIE

Jalousie means 'shutter' in French, and the traditional slatted puff pastry topping of this fruit pie looks exactly like the shutters which adorn the windows of French houses.

───── INGREDIENTS ─────

Serves 4

225g/8oz ready-made puff pastry
a little beaten egg
90ml/6 tbsp apricot conserve
30ml/2 tbsp caster sugar
30ml/2 tbsp flaked almonds
cream or natural yogurt, to serve

1 Preheat the oven to 220°C/425°F/ Gas 7. Roll out the pastry on a lightly floured surface and cut into a 30cm/12in square. Cut in half to make two rectangles.

2 Place one piece of pastry on a wetted baking sheet and brush all round the edges with beaten egg. Spread over the apricot conserve.

3 Fold the remaining rectangle in half lengthways and cut about eight diagonal slits from the centre fold to within about 1cm/½in from the edge all the way along.

4 Unfold the pastry and lay it on top of the conserve covered pastry on the baking sheet. Press the pastry edges together well to seal and knock up with the back of a knife.

5 Brush the slashed pastry with water and sprinkle over the caster sugar and flaked almonds.

6 Bake in the oven for 25–30 minutes, until well risen and golden brown. Remove the jalousie from the oven and leave to cool. Serve sliced, with cream or natural yogurt.

COOK'S TIP
Use other flavours of fruit conserve to fill the jalousie, or if you prefer, substitute some canned fruit pie filling instead. You could also make smaller, individual jalousies to serve with morning coffee, if you like.

BAKED AMERICAN CHEESECAKE

INGREDIENTS

Makes 9 squares

For the base

*175g/6oz/1½ cups crushed sweetmeal
    biscuits*

40g/1½oz/3 tbsp butter, melted

For the topping

*450g/1lb/2½ cups curd cheese or full fat
    soft cheese*

115g/4oz/½ cup caster sugar

3 eggs

finely grated rind of 1 lemon

15ml/1 tbsp lemon juice

2.5ml/½ tsp vanilla essence

15ml/1 tbsp cornflour

30ml/2 tbsp soured cream

*150ml/¼ pint/⅔ cup soured cream and
    1.25ml/¼ tsp ground cinnamon, to
    decorate*

1 Preheat the oven to 170°C/325°F/
Gas 3. Lightly grease and line an
18cm/7in square loose-based tin.

2 Place the crushed biscuits and butter
in a bowl and mix well. Tip into the
base of the prepared cake tin and press
down firmly with a potato masher.

3 Place the cheese in a bowl, add the
sugar and beat well until smooth.
Add the eggs one at a time, beating well
after each addition and then stir in the
lemon rind and juice, the vanilla
essence, cornflour and soured cream.
Beat until smooth.

4 Pour the mixture on to the biscuit
base and level out. Bake for 1¼
hours, or until the cheesecake has set in
the centre. Turn off the oven and leave
inside until completely cold.

5 Remove the cheesecake from the tin,
top with the soured cream and swirl
with the back of a spoon. Sprinkle with
cinnamon and cut into squares.

MANGO ICE CREAM

Mangoes are used widely in Far Eastern cooking, particularly in Thailand, where they are used to make this deliciously rich and creamy ice cream.

INGREDIENTS

Serves 4-6
2 x 425g/15oz cans sliced mango, drained
50g/2oz/4 tbsp caster sugar
30ml/2 tbsp lime juice
15ml/1 tbsp powdered gelatine
350ml/12fl oz/1½ cups double cream, lightly whipped
fresh mint sprigs, to decorate

1 Reserve four slices of mango for decoration and chop the remainder. Place the mangoes in a bowl with the sugar and lime juice.

2 Put 45ml/3 tbsp hot water in a small bowl and sprinkle over the gelatine. Place over a pan of gently simmering water and stir until dissolved. Pour on to the mangoes and mix well.

3 Add the lightly whipped cream and fold into the mango mixture. Pour the mixture into a polythene freezer container and freeze until half frozen.

4 Place in a food processor or blender and blend until smooth. Spoon back into the container and re-freeze.

5 Remove from the freezer 10 minutes before serving and place in the fridge. Serve scoops of ice cream decorated with pieces of the reserved sliced mango and fresh mint.

Greek Fig and Honey Pudding

A quick and easy pudding made from fresh or canned figs topped with thick and creamy Greek yogurt, drizzled with honey and sprinkled with pistachio nuts.

──────── INGREDIENTS ────────

Serves 4

4 fresh or canned figs
2 x 223g/8oz tubs/2 cups Greek
 strained yogurt
60ml/4 tbsp clear honey
30ml/2 tbsp chopped pistachio
 nuts

1 Chop the figs and place in the bottom of four stemmed glasses or deep, individual dessert bowls.

2 Top each glass or bowl of figs with half a tub (½ cup) of the Greek yogurt. Chill until ready to serve.

3 Just before serving drizzle 15ml/1 tbsp of honey over each one and sprinkle with the pistachio nuts.

COOK'S TIP
Look out for specialist honeys made from the nectar of flowers like lavender, clover, acacia, heather, rosemary and thyme.

Russian Fruit Compôte

This fruit pudding is traditionally called *Kissel* and is made from the thickened juice of stewed red or blackcurrants. This recipe uses the whole fruit with added blackberry liqueur.

──────── INGREDIENTS ────────

Serves 4

225g/8oz/2 cups red or blackcurrants
 or a mixture of both
225g/8oz/2 cups raspberries
150ml/5fl oz/⅔ cup water
50g/2oz/4 tbsp caster sugar
22.5ml/1½ tbsp arrowroot
15–30ml/1–2 tbsp Crème de Mûre
Greek yogurt, to serve

1 Place the red or blackcurrants and raspberries, water and sugar in a pan. Cover the pan and cook gently over a low heat for 12–15 minutes, until the fruit is soft.

2 Blend the arrowroot with a little water in a small bowl and stir into the hot fruit mixture. Bring the fruit mixture back to the boil, stirring all the time until thickened and smooth.

3 Remove the pan from the heat and leave the fruit compôte to cool slightly, then gently stir in the Crème de Mûre.

4 Pour the compôte into four glass serving bowls and leave until cold, then chill until required. Serve topped with spoonfuls of Greek yogurt.

COOK'S TIP
Crème de Mûre is a blackberry liqueur available from large supermarkets – you could use Crème de Cassis instead, if you prefer.

MISSISSIPPI PECAN PIE

Makes a 20cm/8in pie

For the pastry
115g/4oz/1 cup plain flour
50g/2oz/4 tbsp butter, cubed
25g/1oz/2 tbsp caster sugar
1 egg yolk

For the filling
175g/6oz/5 tbsp golden syrup
50g/2oz/⅓ cup dark muscovado
* sugar*
50g/2oz/4 tbsp butter
3 eggs, lightly beaten
2.5ml/½ tsp vanilla essence
150g/5oz/1¼ cups pecan nuts
fresh cream or ice cream, to serve

1 Place the flour in a bowl and add the butter. Rub in with your fingertips until the mixture resembles breadcrumbs, then stir in the sugar, egg yolk and about 30ml/2 tbsp cold water. Mix to a dough and knead lightly on a floured surface until smooth.

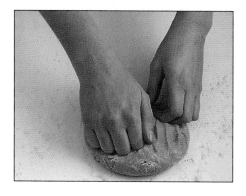

2 Roll out the pastry and use to line a 20cm/8in loose-based fluted flan tin. Prick the base, then line with greaseproof paper and fill with baking beans. Chill for 30 minutes. Preheat the oven to 200°C/400°F/Gas 6.

3 Bake the pastry case for 10 minutes. Remove the paper and beans and bake for 5 minutes. Reduce the oven temperature to 180°C/350°F/Gas 4.

4 Meanwhile, heat the syrup, sugar and butter in a pan until the sugar dissolves. Remove from the heat and cool slightly. Whisk in the eggs and vanilla essence and stir in the pecans.

5 Pour into the pastry case and bake for 35–40 minutes, until the filling is set. Serve with cream or ice cream.

BOSTON BANOFFEE PIE

——— INGREDIENTS ———

Makes a 20cm/8in pie
150g/5oz/1¼ cups plain flour
225g/8oz/1 cup butter
50g/2oz/4 tbsp caster sugar
½ x 405g/14oz can skimmed, sweetened
*   condensed milk*
115g/4oz/⅔ cup soft light brown sugar
30ml/2 tbsp golden syrup
2 small bananas, sliced
a little lemon juice
whipped cream, to decorate
5ml/1 tsp grated plain chocolate

1 Preheat the oven to 160°C/325°F/ Gas 3. Place the flour and 115g/4oz/ ½ cup of the butter in a food processor and blend until crumbed (or rub in with your fingertips). Stir in the caster sugar.

2 Squeeze the mixture together with your hands until it forms a dough. Press into the base of a 20cm/8in loose-based fluted flan tin. Bake for 25–30 minutes, until lightly browned.

3 Place the remaining 115g/4oz/½ cup butter with the condensed milk, brown sugar and golden syrup into a non-stick saucepan and heat gently, stirring, until the butter has melted and the sugar dissolved.

4 Bring to a gentle boil and cook for 7 minutes, stirring all the time (to prevent burning), until the mixture thickens and turns a light caramel colour. Pour on to the cooked pastry base and leave until cold.

5 Sprinkle the bananas with lemon juice and arrange in overlapping circles on top of the caramel filling, leaving a gap in the centre. Pipe a swirl of whipped cream in the centre and sprinkle with the grated chocolate.

APRICOTS WITH ORANGE CREAM

Mascarpone is a very rich cream cheese made from thick Lombardy cream. It is delicious flavoured with orange as a topping for these poached, chilled apricots.

———— INGREDIENTS ————

Serves 4
450g/1lb/2½ cups ready-to-eat dried apricots
strip of lemon peel
1 cinnamon stick
25g/1oz/2 tbsp caster sugar
150ml/¼ pint/⅔ cup sweet dessert wine (such as Muscat de Beaumes de Venise)
115g/4oz/½ cup Mascarpone cream cheese
45ml/3 tbsp orange juice
10ml/2 tsp caster sugar
pinch of ground cinnamon and fresh mint sprig, to decorate

1 Place the apricots, lemon peel and cinnamon stick in a pan and cover with 450ml/¾ pint/1⅞ cups cold water. Bring to the boil, cover and then simmer gently for 25 minutes, until the fruit is tender.

2 Remove from the heat and stir in the dessert wine. Leave until cold, then chill for 3–4 hours or overnight.

3 Mix together the Mascarpone cheese, orange juice and sugar in a bowl and beat well until smooth. Chill until required.

4 Just before serving remove the cinnamon stick and lemon peel from the apricots and serve with a spoonful of the chilled Mascarpone orange cream sprinkled with a little cinnamon and decorated with a sprig of fresh mint.

RHUBARB AND ORANGE FOOL

Perhaps this traditional English pudding got its name because it is so easy to make that even a 'fool' can attempt it.

———— INGREDIENTS ————

Serves 4
30ml/2 tbsp orange juice
5ml/1 tsp finely pared orange rind
1kg/2lb (about 10–12 stems) rhubarb, chopped
15ml/1 tbsp redcurrant jelly
45ml/3 tbsp caster sugar
150g/5oz pot ready-to-serve thick and creamy custard
150ml/¼ pint/⅔ cup double cream
sweet biscuits, to serve

1 Place the orange juice and rind, the rhubarb, redcurrant jelly and sugar into a saucepan. Cover and simmer gently for about 8 minutes, stirring occasionally, until the rhubarb is just tender but not mushy.

2 Remove the pan from the heat, transfer the rhubarb to a bowl and leave to cool completely. Meanwhile, beat the cream lightly.

3 Drain the cooled rhubarb to remove some of the liquid. Reserve about 30ml/2 tbsp of the rhubarb and a little orange rind for decoration. Purée the remaining rhubarb in a food processor or blender, or push through a sieve.

4 Stir the custard into the purée, then fold in the whipped cream. Spoon the fool into individual bowls, cover and chill. Just before serving, top with the reserved fruit and rind. Serve with crisp, sweet biscuits.

RIPPLED CHOCOLATE ICE CREAM

Rich, smooth and packed with chocolate, this heavenly ice cream is an all-round-the-world chocoholics' favourite – and it's so easy to make.

INGREDIENTS

Serves 4

60ml/4 tbsp chocolate and hazelnut spread
450ml/¾ pint/1⅞ cups double cream
15ml/1 tbsp icing sugar, sifted
50g/2oz/5 tbsp chopped plain chocolate
plain chocolate curls, to decorate

1 Mix together the chocolate and hazelnut spread and 75ml/5 tbsp of the double cream in a bowl.

2 Place the remaining cream and the icing sugar in a second bowl and beat until softly whipped.

3 Lightly fold in the chocolate mixture with the chopped chocolate until the mixture is rippled. Transfer to a polythene freezer container and freeze for about 3–4 hours, until firm.

4 Remove the ice cream from the freezer about 10 minutes before serving to allow it to soften slightly. Spoon or scoop into dessert dishes or glasses and top each serving with a few plain chocolate curls.

ORANGES WITH SAFFRON YOGURT

After a hot and spicy curry, a popular Indian pudding is simply sliced, juicy oranges sprinkled with a little cinnamon and served with a spoonful of saffron-flavoured yogurt.

INGREDIENTS

Serves 4

4 large oranges
1.25ml/¼ tsp ground cinnamon
150g/5oz carton natural yogurt
10ml/2 tsp caster sugar
3–4 saffron strands
1.25ml/¼ tsp ground ginger
15ml/1 tbsp chopped pistachio nuts, toasted
fresh lemon balm or mint leaves, to decorate

> COOK'S TIP
> If you haven't any oranges to hand, you could use clementines or the deliciously juicy blood oranges when they are in season.

1 Slice the bottoms off each of the oranges so they sit upright on a board. Working from the top of the orange, cut across the top and down one side. Follow the contours of the orange to reveal the orange flesh just beneath the pith. Repeat until all the peel and pith has been removed, reserving any juice. Peel the remaining oranges in the same way.

2 Slice the oranges thinly and remove any pips. Lay in a single layer, overlapping the slices, on a shallow serving platter. Sprinkle over the ground cinnamon, then cover and chill.

3 Mix the yogurt, sugar, saffron and ginger together in a bowl and leave to stand for 5 minutes. Spoon into a serving bowl and sprinkle with the nuts. Spoon a little of the yogurt mixture on to each serving and decorate with lemon balm or mint.

CAKES AND BAKES

They always say you leave the best till last, so – if you feel you deserve a tea-time treat – then look no further. When people are asked about their worldwide favourites, American Chocolate Fudge Brownies, and Blueberry Muffins are often top of the list, while cream-filled Chocolate Profiteroles from France come a close second. Other popular bakes include Sticky Gingerbread, a traditional British recipe that is absolutely delicious served still slightly warm. From Holland comes a wonderful deep apple tart with a melt-in-the-mouth pastry, and from Austria comes a delicious raspberry tart; both are hard to resist. If it's something more savoury that you're after, you may find that the Italian Olive Bread will not be allowed to cool down before it is gobbled up.

CLARE'S AMERICAN CARROT CAKE

INGREDIENTS

Makes a 20cm/8in round cake
250ml/8fl oz/1 cup corn oil
175g/6oz/1¼ cups granulated sugar
3 eggs
175g/6oz/1½ cups plain flour
7.5ml/1½ tsp baking powder
7.5ml/1½ tsp bicarbonate of soda
3ml/¾ tsp salt
7.5ml/1½ tsp ground cinnamon
a good pinch of grated nutmeg
1.25ml/¼ tsp ground ginger
115g/4oz/1 cup chopped walnuts
225g/8oz (2 large) carrots, finely grated
5ml/1 tsp vanilla essence
30ml/2 tbsp soured cream

For the frosting
175g/6oz/1 cup full fat soft cheese
25g/1oz/2 tbsp butter, softened
225g/8oz/2 cups icing sugar, sifted
8 tiny carrots made from orange and
    green coloured marzipan, to decorate

1 Preheat the oven to 180°C/350°F/ Gas 4. Grease two 20cm/8in loose-based round cake tins and line them with greaseproof paper.

2 Put the corn oil and sugar into a bowl and beat well. Add the eggs, one at a time, and beat them very thoroughly into the mixture.

3 Sift the flour, baking powder, bicarbonate of soda, salt, cinnamon and nutmeg into the bowl and beat well. Fold in the chopped walnuts and grated carrots and stir in the vanilla essence and soured cream.

4 Divide the mixture between the prepared tins and bake in the centre of the oven for about 1 hour 5 minutes, or until well risen and springy to touch in the centre (a skewer pierced through the centre should come out clean).

5 Leave to cool in the tin on a wire rack. Meanwhile, mix together all the ingredients for the frosting in a bowl. Beat until smooth.

6 Sandwich the cooled cakes together with a little of the frosting. Spread the remaining frosting over the top of the cake and down the sides, making a swirling pattern with a round-bladed knife. Decorate with the marzipan carrots just before serving.

STICKY GINGERBREAD

INGREDIENTS

Makes 1 loaf
175g/6oz/1½ cups plain flour
10ml/2 tsp ground ginger
2.5ml/½ tsp mixed spice
2.5ml/½ tsp bicarbonate of soda
30ml/2 tbsp black treacle
30ml/2 tbsp golden syrup
75g/3oz/⅛ cup soft dark brown sugar
75g/3oz/6 tbsp butter
1 egg
15ml/1 tbsp milk
15ml/1 tbsp orange juice
2 pieces stem ginger, finely chopped
50g/2oz/½ cup sultanas
5 ready-to-eat apricots, finely chopped
45ml/3 tbsp icing sugar
10ml/2 tsp lemon juice

1 Preheat the oven to 160°C/325°F/ Gas 3. Grease and line a 1kg/2lb loaf tin. Sift the flour, spices and bicarbonate of soda into a bowl.

2 Place the treacle, syrup, sugar and butter in a pan and heat gently until the butter has melted.

3 In a separate small bowl beat the egg, milk and orange juice together.

4 Add the syrup, egg mixture, chopped ginger, sultanas and apricots to the dry ingredients and stir well. Spoon into the prepared tin and level out. Bake in the oven for about 50 minutes, or until the gingerbread is well risen and a skewer pierced through the centre comes out clean.

5 When cooked, remove from the oven, and leave to cool in the tin. Mix the icing sugar with the lemon juice in a bowl and beat until smooth. Drizzle the icing back and forth over the top of the gingerbread, leave to set, then cut into thick slices to serve.

CHOCOLATE PROFITEROLES

These luscious French pastries are often served as a pudding.

INGREDIENTS

Makes 24
65g/2½oz/⅔ cup plain flour
pinch of salt
50g/2oz/4 tbsp butter
2 eggs, beaten
450ml/¾ pint/1⅞ cups whipping cream
115g/4oz plain chocolate

1 Preheat the oven to 220°C/425°F/ Gas 7. Grease two baking sheets. Sift the flour and salt on to a sheet of paper. Put the butter and 150ml/¼ pint/ ⅔ cup water into a pan and heat gently until the butter has melted. Bring to the boil and then tip in the flour all at once.

2 Remove from the heat. Beat until the mixture forms a ball and leaves the sides of the pan. Cool slightly.

3 Gradually add the beaten eggs, beating well after each addition, until a smooth, thick paste is formed. Spoon into a piping bag fitted with a 1cm/½in plain nozzle.

4 Pipe 24 walnut-sized balls on to the baking sheets. Place on the top shelves of the oven and bake for 20–25 minutes, until well risen and golden. Remove and make a slit in each one to allow the steam to escape, then return to the oven for 5 minutes. Cool the profiteroles on a wire rack.

5 Place all but 60ml/4 tbsp of the cream in a bowl, whip until just thick and spoon into a large piping bag fitted with a plain nozzle. Cut each bun in half, fill with cream and reassemble.

6 To make the chocolate sauce, place the chocolate in a pan with 60ml/ 4 tbsp water and the reserved 60ml/ 4 tbsp cream. Heat gently over a very low heat until the chocolate has melted. Serve four to six profiteroles per person on small plates with the hot chocolate sauce poured over.

MEXICAN CINNAMON BISCUITS

Shortbread biscuits called *pastelitos* are traditionally served at Mexican weddings. These little sweet biscuits are dusted with icing sugar to match the bride's wedding dress.

INGREDIENTS

Makes 20
115g/4oz/½ cup butter
25g/1oz/2 tbsp caster sugar
115g/4oz/1 cup plain flour
50g/2oz/½ cup cornflour
1.25ml/¼ tsp ground cinnamon
30ml/2 tbsp chopped mixed nuts
25g/1oz/3 tbsp icing sugar, sifted

1 Preheat the oven to 160°C/325°F/ Gas 3. Lightly grease a baking tray. Place the butter and sugar in a bowl and beat until pale and creamy.

2 Sift in the plain flour, cornflour and cinnamon and gradually work in with a wooden spoon until the mixture comes together. Knead lightly until completely smooth.

3 Take tablespoonfuls of the mixture, roll into 20 small balls and arrange on the baking tray. Press a few chopped nuts into the top of each one and then flatten slightly.

4 Bake the biscuits for about 30–35 minutes, until pale golden. Remove from the oven and, while they are still warm, toss them in the sifted icing sugar. Leave the biscuits to cool on a wire rack before serving.

DUTCH APPLE TART

INGREDIENTS

Makes a 20cm/8in round tart

175g/6oz/1½ cups plain flour
130g/4½oz/9 tbsp butter, cubed and
*   softened*
75g/3oz/6 tbsp caster sugar
pinch of salt
6 medium eating apples, peeled, cored
*   and grated*
50g/2oz/4 tbsp soft light brown sugar
1.25ml/¼ tsp vanilla essence
2.5ml/½ tsp ground cinnamon
25g/1oz/3 tbsp raisins
25g/1oz/4 tbsp flaked almonds, toasted
15ml/1 tbsp caster sugar, for dredging
whipped cream, to serve

1 Preheat the oven to 180°C/350°F/
Gas 4. Lightly butter a 20cm/8in
round springform tin and dust with a
little plain flour.

2 Place the flour in a bowl with the
butter and sugar, then squeeze
together to form a firm dough. Knead
lightly, then wrap and chill for 1 hour.

3 Roll two-thirds of the chilled pastry
out on a lightly floured surface to
form a 25cm/10in round and use to line
the base and two-thirds up the sides of
the tin, pressing the pastry up the sides
with your fingers.

4 Mix together the apples, sugar,
vanilla essence, cinnamon, raisins
and almonds in a bowl. Spoon into the
lined tin and level the surface. Fold the
pastry edge above the level of the
apples down over the filling.

5 Roll out the remaining pastry and
cut into eight 1cm/½in strips. Brush
the strips with cold water and sprinkle
over the caster sugar. Lay on top of the
tart in a lattice, securing the ends to the
folded-over edge with water.

6 Bake in the centre of the oven for 1
hour, or until the pastry is golden.
Remove and leave to cool in the tin.
When the tart is cold, carefully remove
from the tin. Cut into slices and serve
with whipped cream.

BAKLAVA

This sweet and spicy pie from Greece and Turkey is made with layers of buttered filo pastry packed with nuts and sweetened with a honey and lemon syrup.

INGREDIENTS

Makes 10 pieces

75g/3oz/6 tbsp butter, melted
6 large sheets of filo pastry
225g/8oz/2 cups chopped mixed nuts (such as almonds, pistachios, hazelnuts and walnuts)
50g/2oz/1 cup fresh breadcrumbs
5ml/1 tsp ground cinnamon
5ml/1 tsp mixed spice
2.5ml/½ tsp grated nutmeg
250ml/8fl oz/1 cup clear honey
60ml/4 tbsp lemon juice

1 Preheat the oven to 180°C/350°F/ Gas 4. Butter a 18 x 28cm/7 x 11in tin. Unroll the pastry, brush one sheet with melted butter (keep the remainder covered with a dish towel while you work) and use to line the tin, easing it carefully up the sides.

2 Brush two more sheets with butter and lay on top of the base sheet, easing the pastry into the corners and letting the edges overhang.

3 Mix together the nuts, breadcrumbs and spices in a bowl and spoon this mixture into the lined tin.

4 Cut the remaining three sheets of pastry in half widthways and brush each one with a little of the butter. Layer the sheets on top of the filling and fold in any overhanging edges.

5 Top with the remaining buttered sheets. Cut the baklava diagonally into diamonds. Bake in the oven for about 30 minutes, until golden.

6 Meanwhile, heat the honey and lemon juice together in a pan. When the baklava is cooked, remove from the oven and pour the syrup over while still warm. Leave to cool completely, re-cut into diamonds and serve.

BLUEBERRY MUFFINS

Hot blueberry muffins with a hint of vanilla are an American favourite for breakfast, a mid-morning snack or tea. Make a batch with your children – you'll find that they will love to help cook – and eat – them.

INGREDIENTS

Makes 12
350g/12oz/3 cups plain flour
10ml/2 tsp baking powder
1.25ml/¼ tsp salt
115g/4oz/½ cup caster sugar
2 eggs, beaten
300ml/½ pint/1¼ cups milk
115g/4oz/½ cup butter, melted
5ml/1 tsp vanilla essence
175g/6oz/1⅓ cups blueberries

1 Preheat the oven to 200°C/400°F/ Gas 6. Grease a 12 hole muffin tray.

2 Sift the flour, baking powder and salt into a large mixing bowl and stir in the sugar.

3 Place the eggs, milk, butter and vanilla essence in a separate bowl and whisk together well.

4 Fold the egg mixture into the dry ingredients with a metal spoon, then gently stir in the blueberries.

5 Spoon the mixture into the muffin holes, filling them until just below the top. Place the muffin tray on the top shelf of the oven and bake for 20–25 minutes, until the muffins are well risen and lightly browned. Leave the muffins in the tray for 5 minutes and then turn them out on to a wire rack to cool. Serve warm or cold.

AMERICAN CHOCOLATE FUDGE BROWNIES

INGREDIENTS

Makes 12 pieces
175g/6oz/¾ cup butter
40g/1½oz/6 tbsp cocoa powder
2 eggs, lightly beaten
175g/6oz/1¼ cups soft light brown sugar
2.5ml/½ tsp vanilla essence
115g/4oz/1 cup chopped pecan nuts
50g/2oz/½ cup self-raising flour

For the frosting
115g/4oz plain chocolate
25g/1oz/2 tbsp butter
15ml/1 tbsp soured cream

1 Preheat the oven to 180°C/350°F/ Gas 4. Grease and line a 20cm/8in square, shallow cake tin with grease-proof paper. Melt the butter in a pan and stir in the cocoa.

2 Beat together the eggs, sugar and vanilla essence in a bowl, then stir in the cooled cocoa mixture with the nuts. Sift over the flour and fold into the mixture with a metal spoon.

3 Pour the mixture into the prepared tin and bake for 30–35 minutes, until risen. Remove from the oven (the mixture will still be quite soft and wet, but it cooks further on cooling) and leave to cool in the tin.

4 To make the frosting, melt the chocolate and butter together in a pan and remove from the heat. Beat in the soured cream until smooth and glossy. Leave to cool slightly and then spread over the top of the brownies. When set, cut into twelve pieces.

ITALIAN OLIVE BREAD

A traditional Italian bread called *Focaccia* made with olive oil and flavoured with a Mediterranean mixture of olives, sun-dried tomatoes and dried thyme.

─────── INGREDIENTS ───────

Makes 1 loaf
350g/12oz/3 cups strong plain flour
2.5ml/½ tsp salt
5ml/1 tsp easy-blend dried yeast
5ml/1 tsp dried thyme
45ml/3 tbsp olive oil
4 black olives, stoned and chopped
3 sun-dried tomatoes in oil, chopped
crushed rock salt

1 Place the flour and salt in a bowl and sprinkle over the yeast and thyme. Make a well in the centre and pour in 200ml/7fl oz/⅞ cup of warm water and 30ml/2 tbsp of the olive oil.

2 Mix to a dough and knead on a floured surface for 10 minutes, until elastic (or use a food processor or a mixer with a dough attachment).

3 Place the dough in a large oiled polythene bag. Seal and leave in a warm place for about 2 hours, or until the dough has doubled in size.

4 Turn out the dough on a floured surface and knead lightly. Flatten with your hands. Sprinkle over the olives and tomatoes and knead in until well distributed. Shape the dough into a long oval and place on a greased baking sheet. Cover and leave to rise in a warm place for 45 minutes. Preheat the oven to 190°C/375°F/Gas 5.

5 When risen, press your finger several times into the dough, drizzle over the remaining olive oil and sprinkle with the salt. Bake for 35–40 minutes, until the loaf is golden and sounds hollow when tapped on the bottom.

COURGETTE AND PARMESAN BREAD

Vegetable breads made with baking powder are popular in Australia, America and in Great Britain, too. They are a delicious way to use up a glut of home-grown produce.

INGREDIENTS

Makes 1 loaf
150g/5oz/1¼ cups plain flour
150g/5oz/1 cup wholemeal flour
10ml/2 tsp baking powder
5ml/1 tsp salt
5ml/1 tsp ground cumin
5ml/1 tsp fennel seeds
225g/8oz (2 medium) courgettes, grated
150ml/¼ pint/⅔ cup vegetable oil
2 eggs, beaten
45ml/3 tbsp milk
50g/2oz/⅔ cup grated Parmesan cheese
5ml/1 tsp sesame seeds
salt and black pepper

1 Preheat the oven to 180°C/350°F/ Gas 4. Grease a 1kg/2lb loaf tin and line the base. Sift the flours, baking powder, salt and cumin into a bowl and tip in any bran left in the sieve.

2 Add the fennel seeds, followed by the grated courgette.

3 Whisk together the oil, eggs, milk and half the cheese in a bowl. Stir into the courgette mixture.

4 Spoon the mixture into the prepared tin and level the top. Sprinkle the top with the remaining Parmesan cheese. Bake for 40–45 minutes, until risen and when a skewer pierced through the centre comes out clean. Serve hot or cold.

WELSH CAKES

Pice ar y Maen – cakes on the stone or Welsh cakes – are fruity, spiced teacakes traditionally cooked on a bakestone. They are served warm as a popular teatime treat all over Wales.

INGREDIENTS

Makes 12
225g/8oz/2 cups plain flour
2.5ml/½ tsp baking powder
5ml/1 tsp mixed spice
50g/2oz/4 tbsp butter
50g/2oz/4 tbsp lard
75g/3oz/6 tbsp caster sugar, plus
  15ml/1 tbsp extra for sprinkling
50g/2oz/½ cup raisins or currants
1 egg, beaten
5ml/1 tbsp milk

1 Sift the flour, baking powder and mixed spice into a bowl. Add the butter and lard and rub in with your fingertips until the mixture resembles fine breadcrumbs.

2 Stir in the sugar and the raisins or currants and mix well. Add the egg and milk and mix to form a soft dough. Knead lightly, then roll out the dough on a lightly floured surface to a 5mm/¼in thickness. Cut into twelve 6cm/2½in rounds with a fluted cutter.

3 Lightly grease a large heavy-based frying pan or griddle and cook the cakes in batches on a low to medium heat for about 4–5 minutes each side, until golden brown and cooked, yet still moist in the centre. Sprinkle the cakes with caster sugar while still warm and serve at once.

AUSTRIAN RASPBERRY TART

INGREDIENTS

Makes a 23cm/9in tart
150g/5oz/1¼ cups plain flour
1.25ml/¼ tsp ground cinnamon
1.25ml/¼ tsp ground allspice
pinch of grated nutmeg
75g/3oz/1 cup roasted hazelnuts,
  ground
75g/3oz/6 tbsp butter, diced
50g/2oz/4 tbsp caster sugar
2 egg yolks
135ml/9 tbsp raspberry jam
icing sugar, for dusting
raspberries and fresh mint sprigs, to
  decorate
cream to serve

1 Sift the flour and spices into a bowl and stir in the ground hazelnuts. Rub the butter into the flour until the mixture resembles fine breadcrumbs (or use a food processor).

2 Stir in the caster sugar and add the egg yolks. Squeeze together until a dough is formed and knead lightly. Wrap and chill for about 30 minutes. Meanwhile, preheat the oven to 180°C/350°F/Gas 4.

3 Roll out the pastry and use to line a 20cm/8in loose-based flan tin. Prick the base. Re-roll the pastry trimmings and cut into 5mm/¼in wide strips.

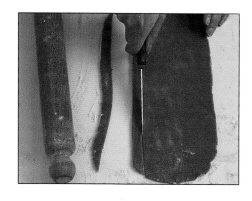

4 Spread the jam over the base, top with a lattice of the pastry strips, pressing the ends on to the edge of the tart with your fingers.

5 Bake for 35–40 minutes until dark golden. Dust the tart with icing sugar while still warm, decorate with raspberries and fresh mint sprigs and serve with cream.

PEANUT BUTTER COOKIES

Peanut butter is probably the most favourite American spread. These cookies are so easy to make and delicious to eat!

INGREDIENTS

Makes 15 cookies
115g/4oz/½ cup butter, softened
115g/4oz/⅝ cup soft light brown sugar
45ml/3 tbsp crunchy peanut butter
1 egg, lightly beaten
2.5ml/½ tsp vanilla essence
200g/7oz/1¾ cups plain flour
2.5ml/½ tsp baking powder
25g/1oz/¼ cup honey roast peanuts,
  chopped

1 Preheat the oven to 180°C/350°F/ Gas 4. Grease two baking sheets. Place the butter, sugar and peanut butter in a bowl and beat until light brown and creamy (or use a food processor).

2 Add the egg and vanilla essence and beat in well. Sift the flour and baking powder into the bowl and mix with a wooden spoon until crumbly. Mix together with your hands to form a dough and knead lightly on a floured surface until smooth.

3 Break off 15 pieces of the dough and roll into balls. Place on the baking sheets and flatten slightly.

4 Press a few pieces of the honey roast peanuts into the top of each one and bake in the oven for 10–12 minutes, until just golden.

5 Remove the cookies from the oven, leave for 1 minute to firm slightly and then transfer with a palette knife to a wire rack to cool.

ITALIAN PASTRY TWISTS

Deep-fried pastry twists, hearts or knots traditionally flavoured with Vin Santo, a sherry-like Italian wine, are served hot, dusted with icing sugar, at Italian carnival time.

INGREDIENTS

Makes about 40
250g/9oz/2¼ cups plain flour
1 egg
pinch of salt
25g/1oz/2 tbsp granulated sugar
2.5ml/½ tsp vanilla essence
25g/1oz/2 tbsp butter, melted
45–60ml/3–4 tbsp sherry
oil, for deep-frying
icing sugar, for dusting

1 Sift the flour into a large mixing bowl and make a well in the centre. Add the egg, salt, sugar, vanilla essence and melted butter.

2 Mix with your hands until the mixture starts to come together. When the dough becomes stiff, add enough sherry to make the dough soft and pliable. Knead until smooth and then wrap and chill for about 1 hour.

3 Roll out the pastry thinly and cut into forty 18 x 1cm/7 x ½in strips. Tie each one loosely into a knot.

4 Heat the oil in a pan to 190°C/ 375°F and deep-fry the knots in batches for 2–3 minutes, until puffed up and golden.

5 Drain the pastry twists on kitchen paper, sprinkle them generously with icing sugar and serve either hot or cold with coffee.

INDEX